MAKING SENSE

The Meaning of a Life

MAKING SENSE
The Meaning of a Life

Joseph Fabry

Skinner House Books
Boston

Published by Skinner House Books, an imprint of the Unitarian Universalist Association, 25 Beacon Street, Boston, MA 02108-2800.

Printed in Canada.

Cover design: Suzanne Morgan
Text design: DeNee Reiton Skipper

ISBN 1-55896-406-1

10 9 8 7 6 5 4 3 2 1
05 04 03 02 01 00

In my belief, every human being has a personal religion, and every community has a collective religion, whether the person or community is aware of this or not. . . . Spiritual nature, like physical nature, abhors a vacuum, If we succeed in repudiating the religion that we have inherited, we shall inevitably acquire a substitute for it.

ARNOLD TOYNBEE

For the naive man, God is a being from whose care one hopes to benefit and whose punishment one fears; a sublimation of a feeling similar to that of a child for its father.

But the scientist is possessed by the sense of universal causation. . . . His religious feeling takes the form of a rapturous amazement at the harmony of natural law, which reveals an intelligence of such superiority that, compared with it, all the systematic thinking and acting of human beings is an utterly insignificant reflection.

ALBERT EINSTEIN

Life must be lived forwards
but can only be understood backwards.

SOREN KIERKEGAARD

Table of Contents

Preface

In January 1998, my father started working on the manuscript which was to become his last book. He had a sense of urgency and excitement about getting his ideas down on paper. A computer problem which delayed the start of his writing added some frustration to the urgency. He rewrote the manuscript several times in response to feedback which suggested a more personal and less intellectual approach. The final revision emphasizes the personal and offers the reader much to think about.

When I read this book, my dad sounded like a man carrying much pain mixed with great joy and optimism. In my relationship with my dad, I rarely saw the pain. As a child, I didn't hear about Hitler until I learned about the Holocaust in school. I didn't realize what I had missed in not knowing my grandparents, who died in the Holocaust, until I saw my children's lives enriched by their grandparents. My dad treasured things that many of us take for granted—the freedom in America, the right to vote, the joy of being part of a family and of having descendants.

I noticed his optimistic outlook when he took us to see the apartment he grew up in in Vienna. After we left, he commented on how different the apartment looked. There was only one thing he recognized from his childhood, the ceramic furnace. I thought he might feel disappointed, but he said he liked the improvements.

My dad had a tremendous curiosity about the future. Although he was not mechanically gifted, he was fascinated by new inventions and eager to try out the ones that could enrich his life. He referred to his computer as "My darling Macintosh." He looked forward to getting an e-mail address and learning about web sites. Unfortunately on the day that he was going to get e-mail on his computer, he had a small heart attack, which started a steady decline in his health.

His ultimate test was to apply Logotherapy, a theory of psychotherapy developed by Viktor Frankl, to the final months of his life. This was hard because he loved being alive. He accepted his fate by treasuring his visits with family and close friends. Many people told him in person or by letter how he had enriched their lives. This meant a lot to him. I think he felt satisfied that he had lived a long, productive, and fulfilling life. His curiosity about the future was with him until the end. In my last conversation with my dad, he asked me, "What do you think will happen in the next three years?"

I am happy that you will get to know my dad by reading this book. I hope that it enriches your life and inspires you to see your life challenges in a new and positive way.

—Claire Fabry Bradley

Introduction

Congratulations, dear reader, you are a survivor. And it wasn't always easy.

You have survived your childhood traumas, the damage inflicted to your self-image, intentionally or unwittingly, by parents, teachers, schoolmates, and peers, the self-doubts of your teenage years, the disappointments of puppy love, the sicknesses and accidents, the midlife crisis, the burnout, the blows of fate, the loss of dear ones, the physical handicaps and emotional burdens. You have survived all that, and perhaps many more calamities and tragedies.

I have had my share of life's traumas, too, plus the miseries of the Holocaust. Yet, when I look over my life, I am puzzled. If, at the time of my birth, I had been able to see my future life and had been asked if I wanted to live through it again, my answer would have been a resounding "No," and I would have crawled back into the womb. Yet, having driven through life and now looking at it through the rear-view mirror, I see less the potholes and traffic accidents and more the magnificent views and challenges. It was a life I wouldn't have wanted to miss.

I have wondered, how is it possible that the same events, while experiencing them, are so painful and, seen in retrospect, so fulfilling? I let my life pass by my inner eyes, as it allegedly does before death. The film of my life is now in its last reel, and I see connections I had overlooked, misunderstood, or misinterpreted. I see disasters as teachers, frustrations as challenges, crises as opportunities.

In this book I am telling the story of a man who has arrived at a reasoned and optimistic faith in spite of having lived through one of the worst tragedies, the Holocaust, as well as the more familiar perplexities and torments of life: adolescent sexual fears, the crises of staleness in career and marriage, conflicts about religious identity, the self-doubt of a parent when offspring opt for religious groups at odds with one's own, children whose counterculture beliefs and lifestyle demand a reevaluation of one's own belief, and finally the murder of a daughter, the kind of violence that more and more every parent dreads and wonders how to survive.

I do not claim that my understanding of life is for everybody. Quite the contrary. I am convinced that every person has to find his or her own answers. People may accept the guidelines of existing religions, or struggle to find guidelines that make sense to them within their personal experiences.

I know now that no step in my life's journey has been in vain, not even those that were hurtful or frustrating. Storming against the impenetrable wall of an unavoidable fate resulted only in a bloody head. Where fate was avoidable, I sometimes was able to find openings in that wall, sometimes not. I learned to fight what could be changed and to accept what couldn't. A Japanese friend told me a fitting metaphor: If you are in a cage with a powerful but good-natured bull, try to get along with it; but if you are caged up with a small poisonous snake, try to kill it.

Only now, when I am close to seeing my life in its totality does it make sense to me. During most of the time it looked to me like the back of a carpet with zillions of tiny threads in random patterns that were arranged in apparent chaos. Only now when the weaving is almost finished, and I turn the carpet of my life around, can I see its harmonious pattern. It's no longer a jumble of confusion with lots of loose ends. I can see the design.

Reality, in weaving the story of our lives, does not guarantee happy endings, and no reweaving is possible. At every moment, we constantly turn potentials into actualities. But while a reweaving of the unhappy parts of my life is impossible, the imagination is free. I have been blessed with a vivid imagination. I have found it a healthy exercise to rewrite some episodes in my fantasy in the way I would have liked them to come out. I have included these imagined happy endings in my otherwise factual account.

As the Viennese psychotherapist Viktor Frankl, one of my most influential teachers, has told me many times: "Life is not a Rorschach test, a meaningless blotch into which we can read our own meanings. Rather it is like a 'hidden picture puzzle,' with lines showing clouds, trees, flowers, and people, and a caption that challenges viewers 'to find the bicycle in this picture.' The viewers then need to turn the picture this way and that way, until they find the bicycle in the jumble of lines. In the same way we have to view our lives from all sides until we detect its meaning."

Years in Vienna

The Viennese psychiatrist Alfred Adler says that some clues of our later personality come from our earliest memories. Looking back on my life, I have wondered what in my childhood developed my capacity to draw meaning out of traumas and see order behind chaos. My parents laid the groundwork for my personality—they supplied the soil in which my roots grew and which nourished the tree of my life. Yet, I am amazed how little I know about them—about their true, authentic selves, their innermost feelings, their hopes, doubts, and fears.

I know "facts"—what I observed and what others have told me. I know they both came from families who lived in Sudetenland when it was still part of the Austrian Empire. Their families moved to Vienna in the 1870s after Emperor Francis Joseph granted Jews most of the rights the rest of the Viennese took for granted. My mother finished high school, which was rare for women in those years. My father, who had no education beyond elementary school, began work as an unskilled laborer in the municipal storehouses of Vienna and worked himself up to the directorship.

My mother, Irma Benedikt, was engaged to be married to my father's older brother, David Epstein. A few months before their wedding date, David caught pneumonia and died. My father, Ernst, courted mother and four years later married her.

My mother's engagement and my uncle's death were seldom mentioned in the family, and neither were other misfortunes—a divorce (rare in Jewish families at that time), a mentally retarded cousin, and two cases of insanity.

I know of the tragic event of my uncle's death because my mother kept a souvenir book, as many young women did. In it I found many pages in which David had painted romantic water-colors and written his own poetry. But I never heard my mother voice a single word of regret about marrying my father. As far as I can tell, my parents had a perfect marriage—I never heard them quarrel or even raise their voices at each other, although they had different interests. Mother loved music, poetry, history, and approached life through intuition. Father loved nature, detective stories, politics, card playing, and approached life through logic. Family members and friends came to him for advice. Her sense of humor was gentle; his wit had a sharp edge. She read fairy tales to me; he taught me to play chess.

I never saw them kiss or hug. This was not unusual. Kissing on the mouth was considered unhygienic. Ours was an unkissing, unhugging, untouching family. And yet, it was a loving community that celebrated all holidays and birthdays in somebody's home. There were about twenty-five of us, all in easy commuting distance by streetcar. In addition, there was an inner circle of about a dozen who met every Saturday and Sunday in coffee houses, the women to chat, the men to play Tarock, a card game known only in Austria and Hungary. As the only child, I could choose between the two groups. When I was small, I was an eavesdropper at the women's table. Later I graduated to kibitzer and eventually stand-by with the card players. Members of the inner circle often took summer vacations together at some Alpine lake.

On New Year's Eve, we met in one of mother's cousin's apartments and put on a big show. It was a tongue-in-cheek revue of the family events of the year, songs and sketches about travels, achievements, funny incidents, and also some gentle kidding about mistakes and mishaps. I looked forward to that evening all year. Mother single-handedly sewed the costumes, the artists of the family drew the decorations, wrote the materials, and accompanied songs on the piano. Here, too, I graduated from open-eyed child spectator to writer, singer, and actor.

My earliest memory is walking on a street in Vienna holding my father's hand. We were moving from the apartment where I was born to the apartment where we lived until, twenty-three years later, the Nazi occupation of Austria led to our eviction. I was four at the time. My father and I walked the few blocks to our future home while my mother traveled in the truck that carried our furniture. I think I remember this little scene because of the security I felt holding Father's hand at that moment of change. I often felt the comfort of holding a hand that gave me security in the chaotic changes I was forced to go through. I also remember a sense of curiosity about the new home. I believe that curiosity was part of the saving grace that helped sweeten the dread of the unknown. The sense of curiosity and adventure has never left me during my odyssey.

I was five when Father's mother died. On the morning I was told of her death, I see myself climbing down the stairs from our third-floor apartment taking two little steps for each stair while father walked in front of me. Suddenly I had a thought and said, "Papa, your daddy died a long time ago, and now your mommy is dead, too. Now you are all alone." My father stopped and turned around. He said in a most serious and loving voice, "No, I have you. And you have to be a good boy."

These words were probably the routine answer of a father to a little boy's jabbering, but they live on in me. They must have touched something deep within and placed the seed of responsibleness in me that has never left me. Looking over these eighty-plus years, I am aware that responsibleness has been my constant goal and my burden.

I use the term "responsibleness" rather than the usual "responsibility"; I use "responsibility" when it is dictated by some outside authority, and "responsibleness" when it is self-chosen. A girl who washes the dishes because her mother told her to has been given a responsibility. If she decides to help because her mother is tired after work, she assumes a responsibleness by her own decision.

My first test of responsibleness came soon, when I was six or seven. I had walked to the playground about fifteen minutes away, as every morning, with our maid Minna, a woman of about seventy. At the playground, Minna fainted. When she came to, I took her hand and led her home, carrying her folding chair. I received much praise for this act of early responsibleness and seem to have decided to take care of Minna as much as she took loving care of me. When I was ten, our cook, after visiting her native village near Vienna, came down with the plague, which ravaged the countryside after World War I. Our family, including Minna, was immediately quarantined. After a few days Minna developed a fever. The doctor was about to transfer her to the hospital for infectious diseases, when I pleaded with him to let her stay with us for one more night. In the morning, it was clear that she simply had a cold.

Minna was Catholic. Her religious influence on me did not go much beyond our having a Christmas tree, which she decorated with homemade cookies, apples, and silver-painted walnuts. In my child's mind there was not much difference between the stories about Jacob wrestling with an angel, which I learned in the religious classes in school, the stories about Jesus feeding the multitude with five loaves of bread, which Minna told me, and the fairy tales mother read to me at bedtime. She prayed, went to church, and fingered a rosary. I loved her, and she loved me, and our mutual love, and not any interest in her beliefs, made me occasionally ask her religious questions.

Minna sometimes used words I didn't understand. One of them was "Holy Spirit." It was part of the "Trinity," another word I could not understand. I could visualize God, it was a person, someone like my own father, only more powerful and magical. I could visualize Jesus, he was like a good friend, someone you trusted. But what was the Holy Spirit? I saw it as something like a ghost, but friendly, not scary. I considered it as the least important of the three.

My parents contributed to my lack of fear regarding spiritual matters. My parents and I once visited the cemetery where my father's grandfather was buried. The cemetery was in the newly established Republic of Czechoslovakia. World War I was over, and I was nine years old. The cemetery was closed and surrounded by a high wall with a rusty iron gate, for which we had to get a key. When we finally found the grave, I was delighted to see it covered with red, juicy strawberries. While I helped myself freely, my parents stood by smiling.

It was only much later that I realized what gift they had given me. By not showing disapproval, or even horror, of my eating fruit growing on sacrosanct soil, they made me see the graveyard as a place of serenity and delight. This incident taught my unconscious a precious lesson. It made me see a connectedness and wholeness, where death is not the enemy but part of life, and a graveyard is a place where a boy can eat and enjoy berries possibly containing his great-grandfather's chemicals.

When I later struggled with religious concepts, this episode gave me an insight into the mysteries of immortality. Graveyards, ever since, have been places of pleasure rather than dread. We now live next to the Sunset cemetery in El Cerrito, California, where my wife and I have reserved sites. We take relaxed strolls on this magnificent hill with its grand view over the San Francisco Bay.

The Jewishness of my youth was a tender plant. It was a given, like being a male or having blue eyes. Everybody around me was Jewish, but I had little idea what that meant. In school we learned the Hebrew letters. However, at that time Hebrew was a dead language. It was like looking at hieroglyphs. I learned stories about Abraham and Moses, and how they talked to God, and how God performed miracles. All this was removed from my day-to-day life and sounded like fairy tales.

Once a year we attended the Seder meal at my uncle Alois's home. It was a pleasant family gathering, with a lot of joking, singing, and eating. It included readings about still another miracle—this one about freedom. In those pre-Hitler days I had no idea how life-stifling the loss of freedom can be. On Yom Kippur, the Day of Atonement and Reconciliation, we fasted, but I never could think of anyone with whom I needed to reconcile. Only later, the problems of freedom and reconciliation struck me like thunderbolts.

From time to time distant orthodox cousins visited Vienna from the provinces. They wouldn't eat from our plates or turn on the light on Saturday. They refused to carry even the smallest package on Friday evening after they spied the first star in the sky. Once, a very distant relative came from Copenhagen, a rabbi with side locks. He wore a wide-brimmed black hat, even indoors. He wouldn't shake hands with a woman. If this was religion, I could not relate to it.

On my life's journey, walls and mountains have often blocked the way. One of my early problems seems a molehill now, but loomed like the Himalayas: my extreme shyness which became especially painful when I entered the teens and became interested in girls. It seems sacrilegious to say so, but facing my shyness during my teen-age years was as traumatic as later events during the flight for my life. My teen-age years were full of self-doubts and confusion. If I had known about self-actualization, a concept introduced only much later by Abraham Maslow, I wouldn't have known what I wanted to "self-actualize." Was it the boy who fantasized himself as a conquering Douglas Fairbanks, or a shy but wonderful poet like Cyrano, or the sad reality of a boy who had no control over his life, who drifted and followed the decisions of others—parents, teachers, even admired classmates?

The seeds of self-responsibleness were dormant. In retrospect I see that I followed only duties and never assumed responsibleness. The term "inferiority complex" began to be used, even overused, in the Vienna of Alfred Adler. I saw myself as inferior, a shameful failure, in spite of the fact that my parents and other family members praised me for every, even the tiniest, achievement. Only cousin Gretl spoke to me in a different tone. She was thirteen years older and married to my cousin Arthur, who was a newspaperman and my idol. "You are spoiled rotten," she would tell me, "and never will amount to anything."

I suspected that she was the only one who really knew me, that she could see through the phoniness of my accomplishments in school, in sports, in writing poetry. I thought she alone knew my authentic self and told me the truth. I mistrusted the praise of others and believed her cruel honesty.

During college, the circle of important people in my life grew to include my life-long friend Max. I have known many people whom I called "friends," but in the last analysis they remained friends in quotation marks only. I have been fortunate to have had Max as a true friend.

I met Max during our studies at the University of Vienna. At that time, the early thirties, the Nazis were illegal in Austria but were allowed to practice their anti-Semitism openly, especially at the University. The University had a "liberal" tradition which did not allow the police into the building and did not interfere with the activities of the students within the building. Some of these activities consisted of beating up Jewish students.

After a few narrow escapes, I did what many students did and not only the Jewish students. Instead of going to the lectures, read in monotonous voices by the professors, we were prepared for the exams by professional note takers. In one of these cramming classes I first met Max, but we really got to know each other later at a spa near Vienna where my uncle took me for a week during summer vacation and where Max tutored the high-school sons of the hotel owner where we stayed.

One evening Max and I went up to the hotel roof terrace to chat. We discovered that we had more in common than the cram courses. Neither of us cared for studying law, which we did only to please our parents. Max told me about his poems that had been published in the youth section of the *Neue Freie Presse,* a boulevard newspaper. I told him about the movie reviews I had written for my cousin Arthur, who was on the staff of another Viennese paper, the *Kronenzeitung.*

We talked until two in the morning. It was instant understanding, with no need for explanations—friendship at first sight. We decided, then and there, to write something together—we didn't know what or how. We only knew that we wanted our writings to be published in the main sections of serious papers.

Viennese newspapers published short short stories of about a thousand words and longer first-hand reports from exotic places. We thought a story of one thousand words should be easy to write. So we sat down at a typewriter. How do two people write one story? We actually tried to write alternate sentences, then alternate paragraphs. The story went in unsuspected directions. We wanted a surprise ending, but not one surprising to us.

About this time Willy Beer, a distant relative, returned from a business trip to New Mexico. He told me about oil discovered on an Indian reservation. New Mexico was exotic enough for Viennese readers, and I wrote a report as Willy had told it to me. Max rewrote it as if he himself had just spoken to the Indian chief. We called the story "Indians as Oil Millionaires." We knew exactly which paper would be interested in this "first-hand" piece of journalism. After we had put it in an envelope, addressed it, and were about to take it to the post office, we realized we had not chosen a by-line.

We wanted one common pen name. We agreed on Peter, a first name popular among young men in Vienna. As a "family" name we chose Fabrizius because we would fabricate our stories, and the Latinized name appealed to us. So the story about the newly-rich Indians went out and was published in 1932 under the pen name Peter Fabrizius.

We wrote and published about 150 short stories and reports between 1932 and 1938, when Hitler ended our career as short-story writers in German, as he ended so much that had filled our lives with meaning.

We developed a method for writing together. One of us had an idea, often grown from tiny seeds. My dog picked up a woman's glove from the gutter. How would it be if the dog led his master to a romantic adventure by sniffing out the owner of the glove? We saw a magician pull masses of streamers, bouquets, flags, and a rabbit out of a small suitcase. What would happen if a thief stole such a suitcase in a bus station and was caught by a policeman who ordered him to open it?

Anything we saw, heard, or imagined triggered a chain of ideas. We spent hours tossing ideas back and forth until we came to a satisfying conclusion and a surprise twist in the last sentence, possibly the last word. While we both were shy, we wrote breezy dialogues and our stories were populated by mischievous young men, hats askew, flirting with dimpled blondes with stunning figures. In our stories we lived the lives we would have liked to live.

Our friendship was rooted in far more than literary cooperation. It was based on an absolute trust which extended to all aspects of life. Later we described our relationship more fully in our autobiography *One and One Make Three*. Together we accomplished much more than the sum of what each of us would have accomplished alone.

We usually tossed a story idea back and forth, but occasionally one of us had a dry period, and then the other took over. The royalties were always divided fifty-fifty, regardless of our share in the work. Sometimes, especially during our summer vacations, one of us wrote a story all by himself. The other one would see it for the first time in a paper under the common pen name. There never was any doubt that payment of even these stories would be divided equally.

During our emigration, Max spent a year in Shanghai while I was in New York. When we finally met in San Francisco, Max pulled an envelope out of his pocket with my share of the royalties he had earned for the stories he had written for the *Shanghai Daily News*. I also had an envelope, containing his share for the stories I had sold in New York. The amounts were so close that we didn't even bother to balance the difference.

Our friendship spread to other common interests—hikes in the Vienna Woods, skiing, theater visits, carnival dances, and long "non-professional" chats about everything under the sun. Oddly, we had different tastes regarding the women we dated. I was attracted by women who were made-up, flashily dressed, with wide-brimmed hats. Max called them "movie stars." He liked simple, nature-loving, plainly dressed girls. I called them "house maid" types. We hardly ever went out as a foursome and never competed for the same girl. Perhaps this was part of the secret of our friendship.

Max and I were together in his parents' apartment on March 13, 1938, when Kurt Schuschnigg announced over the radio his resignation as the chancellor of Austria and Hitler's take-over of Austria.

I believe that among the many painful experiences of our lives every person has at least one decisive trauma. For the older generation it may be the Great Depression. For the younger one, the Vietnam War. For my generation, and for me, it was the Holocaust. On one day, March 13, 1938, when Hitler's troups took over Austria, everything that had been meaningful was taken from me: my family, my friends, my job, my country, and even my language which, as a writer, was vital for a fulfilled life.

Max had foreseen the danger for a Jewish writer in Nazi Austria and had gone to London to establish a Peter Fabrizius foothold there. He had returned to Vienna, but his suitcase was packed for a quick getaway. He left the evening of Schuschnigg's announcement and was able to slip through the immigration check in England before the world closed its borders. It was an adventurous flight which he described later in an article, "The First Swallow." (This article, too, based on his personal experience and written entirely by him, was published under the name of Peter Fabrizius and we shared the royalties.)

I was more naïve politically and stayed in Vienna. After a few days reality set in. Being excluded, despised, and spit upon eroded my self-esteem, which had been undermined by cousin Gretl and recovered by my successes as a short-story writer. I considered myself a piece of flotsam floating on an ocean of uncertainty. Only much later I realized that flotsam can be shaped into pieces of art.

Within days I was reduced from a human being to a cockroach, despised and unwanted. I was abruptly kicked out of my job. Acquaintances, even schoolmates, sported swastikas in their buttonholes and looked the other way when they saw me on the street. When I went to see a movie, the lights went on suddenly, and SS-men stormed in shouting "*Juden raus*!" (Jews get out!). Park benches had signs, "Not for Jews." Stores were marked, "Jews not wanted."

Most humiliations of those days I have blissfully forgotten, but one incident remains stamped in my memory. The Nazi takeover had prevented a planned referendum between the ruling Austrian Christian Democrats and Hitler's National Socialists. The sidewalks and walls were full of graffiti by both parties. I was walking on the street when a car stopped, a brownshirt jumped out and shouted, "Are you a Jew?" When I nodded, he dragged me into the car and drove to one of the government buildings. There a number of men in business suits and women in dresses were on hands and knees scrubbing the anti-Nazi slogans off the sidewalk. I was given a pail and a brush and told to do likewise. A policeman stood by and grinned. Passers-by made abusive remarks and kicked us. One man in overalls came to me, picked up my hand, and shouted, "Look at these soft hands! Never done a day's work in your life. We'll take care of that!" He dropped my hand and spit in my face. The policeman grinned even more broadly, and several passers-by jeered.

It was clearly time to leave Austria. I stood in line for visas at a dozen consulates in Vienna, as did thousands of other Jews. The world was suddenly shut. As tourists we had been welcome, but not as refugees whose lives were at stake.

My father was an inventive man. He had heard that some countries granted short-time visas to people who wanted to transact business there. He bought a patent for a water-saving device for flush toilets, and I applied for permission to enter other countries, not as a refugee but as a businessman. The consuls saw through that ruse and refused the visa.

At that time, Myra, my first lover, had arrived in Brussels. In Vienna, she had been an operetta and cabaret singer. During the depression in Austria, many theaters and nightclubs closed. She couldn't find work in Vienna. An agency arranged engagements for her in the Balkans and North Africa. So we parted. We became penpals when she was abroad and remained lovers on her occasional visits to Vienna. She was quite depressed about her present jobs. Her singing in bars became more and more an excuse for dancing with male guests and persuading them to order wine and to drink with them. She got a percentage of the price of the alcohol consumed. Sexual favors were not part of the written contract, but they were expected. In her letters she made light of these matters, but I knew that this was not the life she wanted. She became quite somber when she talked about her future and more than once predicted, in a voice that had become hoarse from smoking and drinking: "You'll see, Joe. I'll end in the gutter."

In the summer of 1937, on one of her visits to Vienna, where she had a married sister, she told me laughingly of an episode that had happened in a nightclub in Tangier. She had entertained a businessman from Brussels and, after a few drinks, gone to his room with him. While in bed, disgust with her present situation overwhelmed her, and she furiously bit his shoulder. He mistook her rage for passion and, obviously being of that inclination, fell madly in love with her. He wrote her from Brussels asking her to come and live with him. When she refused, he offered marriage. I saw Myra's connection to this man as an opportunity for me to escape Vienna. I asked her to intervene on my behalf, which she did. Her lover wrote to the Belgian consulate in Vienna pretending to be interested in my patent. The consul granted me a one-month entry visa. It took years for me to see the grotesque aspect of the situation. Myra's angry bite, her perverse customer, and a water-saving device for toilets had saved my life—for the time being.

I overstayed my one-month visa and neglected to return to Nazi-occupied Austria, where I would have faced shipment to a concentration camp. Not only was I Jewish but I had also been the editor of a satirical weekly that had published anti-Nazi jokes.

On October 12, 1938, while walking on the streets of Brussels, I was arrested, taken to a police station, photographed, fingerprinted, and taken to a prison. There I was led up steel stairs, through steel corridors, past steel doors, to cell 366. Not until the door clanged shut was I gripped by the enormity of what was happening. I banged against the door shouting, "I am innocent," as Richard Dreyfus did in the movie I had seen only a year before.

Expulsion

As bad as things were in Vienna after the Nazis invaded, I consider my time in the Belgian prison my low point. There were at least a dozen men in that prison whose sole crime was to have escaped from murderers. I saw my fellow inmates only once a day when we were led to the prison courtyard where we marched with the other prisoners in a circle for our daily exercise. The only distinction between us and the convicted criminals was the clothing: they wore prison uniforms; we were allowed to keep our own suits.

We were not permitted to speak to each other, but we managed to whisper a few words. They concerned mostly the rumor that our imprisonment was the first step to our being sent back to Germany, which would have meant our shipment to concentration camps. This rumor was substantiated by the daily disappearance of some of the refugee prisoners from the courtyard and their replacement by others.

Fortunately, most of us avoided the worst because of the intervention of the Bishop of Liege and members of the Jewish Committee in Brussels. They arranged for the Belgian government to set aside part of a vagabond camp for German and Austrian refugees.

This vagabond camp was a social experiment which had existed in Belgium since the early part of the century. The police picked up homeless tramps from the streets and interned them in the camp, where they were put to work for low wages. When they had earned a certain amount of money, they were released. This camp at Merxplas, near the Dutch border, was a little community in itself, with large brick buildings for dormitories, a common kitchen, a church, a hospital, a cemetery, and a railroad connecting the various parts. A few buildings were reserved for us, strictly separated from the rest of the camp. I took it as another proof that we were human refuse.

After two apprehensive weeks in my prison cell, I was allowed three days release before my transport to Merxplas. At one of the low points during my release time, I walked through the streets of Brussels and, exhausted, sat down in a park under a clump of pine trees. My release from prison was under the condition that I agree to be interned in a detention camp, perhaps to be shipped back to Nazi Austria. My country was gone, my parents in peril, my career destroyed, my family and friends scattered, imprisoned, or dead, my future uncertain. I was overcome by despair but suddenly, unexplainedly, a weight lifted—I could face the future, bleak as it was.

The full meaning of this incident became clear to me years later, in the safety of my own home in Berkeley. In a half-dream during the morning waking-up stage, I relived the episode. I saw myself sitting under those pine trees. A sun ray had made its way through the thick branches above me and focused on one of the dead pine twigs on the ground. The twig was perfectly symmetrical, the brown needles on both sides of the stem were in impeccable order, and new light-green growth sprouted from the tip. Because I was now on my religious journey, I could recognize the incident in its full meaning. It was a message from "beyond," from a higher power, assuring me that there still was order in the world. Life was continuing even when death was all around. My unconscious had recognized it as proof that there was a higher power and that it was a higher power that cared.

My arrest was just the first episode in a life that became a succession of traumas, a continual flight from becoming part of Hitler's "final solution." Most of the fifteen others who were taken to Merxplas had a pessimistic outlook, which was confirmed when we arrived at the camp, a bleak place on the heath of northern Belgium. We were the first arrivals of hundreds to come, and the reception by the camp director, in a cold cave of a room with steel-bar windows and wooden benches and tables, confirmed our suspicion that this vagabond camp was little more than a prison.

The uniformed director, with his cylindrical military *chapeau,* read us the regulations. Then we were led to a dormitory room with forty beds lined up against whitewashed walls and no other furniture. I selected one of the bedsteads with its straw mattress and straw pillows and placed my valise and my precious portable typewriter next to it. Then a bell called us to the dining hall where lunch had been brought from the vagabond kitchen. A thin soup, black coffee, and a slice of bread.

"It's a prison," Dr. Bermann diagnosed between spoonfuls. He had been the chief physician of a Vienna hospital.

"In the last, godforsaken corner of this phony social experiment," a hunchback added. He had been a clerk in a Dresden bank. "Here we'll go to rot."

Then another miracle happened. A young attorney from Frankfurt spoke up. I knew him a little because he had shared my daily exercise walks in the prison yard. He was Jakob Benedikt, a name I remembered because it was the same as my maternal grandfather's.

"This will depend on us," Benedikt said. "We will be six hundred. If we pull together, they can't overlook us."

Erwin Neidhart, a union organizer from Berlin, stared at him in surprise, looked around the table, and shook his head. "Pie in the sky," he said.

"We can bring it down to earth and divide it," Benedikt argued. "Tell me one reason why six hundred cannot work together."

"Because they are six hundred."

Benedikt leaned forward, intent with his idea. As he talked his words tumbled from his lips in torrents. As I got to know him better, I loved the youthful enthusiasm that made him speed up his sentences in a telegraph style. Often his words could not keep up with his thoughts, and he began to sputter. His eyes widened and his fingers galloped through the air to emphasize a point.

"We'll either rot here or survive," he bubbled. "We come from different places—manufacturers, professionals, shopkeepers, clerks. We are in the same boat. We can drift or row. Or sink. No use feeling sorry for ourselves."

"Right," Dr. Bermann said. "This vegetating as a refugee makes me sick. Might as well do something."

"You can do a lot as a doctor," Benedikt spoke in staccato. "We cannot start our new lives sick. And we'll have to prepare ourselves. Learn languages. Trades. The world doesn't need German-speaking paper shufflers. It needs farmers and carpenters and auto mechanics who understand English or Spanish."

Hesitatingly, others spoke up. A former businessman said he knew enough English to teach it. Another had been a carpenter apprentice. A third was a boxer and volunteered body work to keep us in shape. I thought about what I could do. Teaching short-story writing in German didn't seem of much use.

"Hey, you," Neidhart called from across the table. "You have a typewriter. How about a weekly newsletter?"

I was surprised how pleased I was when Benedikt added my name to the list he scribbled. I suddenly felt hot and hoped I wasn't blushing. It was a first hint of being Someone and Useful, even if in a very small way.

Then an elderly man spoke up. He had been a judge in Hamburg. He said in a rich, sonorous voice, "What we need are ground rules."

Benedikt looked at him. "Laws? A constitution?"

I was not sure if Judge Stein was being facetious. But he was serious. "Why not? I have often speculated what an ideal constitution for a small democracy would be."

It occurred to me that this would be an idea for a satirical short story. The boxer expressed my thought. "Funny," he said. "The great democracies go to pot, and here we are talking about establishing one in a camp for vagabonds."

In my notebook I found the following comment: "The change is amazing. Like flowers in a meadow, trampled down and rising again after a shower. Dull faces brighten. A purpose. Hope where there was nothing but despair. I feel it myself. To publish a newsletter for a handful of outcasts—what difference does it make? It does make a difference!"

During the next few weeks the camp filled up. Every few days a new busload arrived from Brussels. We interviewed the newcomers for talents. There were carpenters, electricians, cobblers, barbers—Benedikt's list grew. A couple of actors arrived. They volunteered to put on some sketches for us. There was also a youngster with a guitar and a man who had owned a restaurant in Vienna. He made a brave attempt to improve our monotonous meals with the supplies we received from the Belgian government and from the Jewish Committee in Brussels.

The Committee also supplied us with materials for our training classes: an old car to be taken apart, cobbler tools, and electrical wiring. The camp director granted us rights, including cooking our own meals, teaching our own courses, and some self-rule.

Judge Stein wrote our constitution, and we set up a "government." Every dormitory elected a representative for a governing council. Council members were issued gold stars, which they wore with pride on the berets we were issued. We elected a former tax consultant with some experience in politics as "president," and the council members elected "ministers" in charge of various departments such as education, agriculture, retraining, health, the arts, and emigration, which had the almost hopeless task of getting visas. I published my newsletter with the help of seventeen-year-old Kurt Goldner, a high-school student who was a gifted cartoonist. Three carbon copies were posted on the bulletin boards, one in each dormitory building.

Yes, it looks like a success story in retrospect, and in its unique way, it was a success story. However while I was there, camp life often seemed unbearable. Six hundred men were crammed into three massive brick barracks, their nerves raw from the desperate news they received from those left behind. And there seemed to be no future.

There was never a moment of privacy from the six o'clock wake-up call, when we were herded in the dark, freezing winter mornings across the soccer field to the giant washroom (cold water only), until the nine o'clock night call. During the day we were not allowed to go to the dormitories and rest on our beds. We had to spend hours in the overcrowded day room with its iron stoves, which were kept going by our own crew. The wood delivered to us was never enough. I remember the day when the head of our crew, a professor from the University of Freiburg, agonized about having to burn some books from the camp library—an episode preserved in a cartoon by young Kurt Goldner in my weekly bulletin.

There was no privacy even on the toilets, which were a row of doorless stinkholes in the open and without water. The meals in the giant dining hall were sometimes interrupted by ugly demonstrations about the monotony of the food, which even the wizardry of the Viennese restaurateur could not make palatable. Dr. Bermann, with whom I formed a special friendship, tried in vain to get an extra room for the sick, but they had to remain in their dormitory beds with the others. Bermann, his assistants, and a pharmacist from Stuttgart had to get by with the skimpiest supply of medicines.

The worst part was the continual stream of news from home about relatives shipped to concentration camps, and the desperate pleas for help. But we were helpless ourselves. Our "department of emigration" was not very successful. It consisted of three frustrated men who had some knowledge of languages and who kept up correspondence with consulates and with the Jewish committee in Brussels, which also tried to get visas. During my stay in Merxplas, only a handful of inmates received permission to enter overseas countries.

When I later succeeded, with Max's help, in getting to England, I wrote a manuscript from the notes I had taken at Merxplas. It was a bitter accusation of a world that had shut its doors. I gave it the title, "No Room for Six Hundred." The manuscript was never published. I was surprised at my shift of view when I reread the manuscript in the 1980s. As I remembered Merxplas with the hindsight of forty years, my old manuscript no longer seemed a description of despair but a testimony to what humans are capable of accomplishing, even under hopeless conditions. The revised book was published in 1991 under the title *The Next-to-Final Solution*. I chose this title because by then I knew that most of my unfortunate comrades had become victims of the "final solution" in German concentration camps after the Nazis overran Belgium in 1940.

What stands out in my mind about Merxplas is our stubborn attempt to take our fate in our hands and our refusal to feel like helpless victims of a situation over which we had no control. We tried to establish an organized community within a camp for tramps, to find a purpose in a world drifting in turmoil. That this short-lived effort was swallowed up by the tidal wave of history didn't detract from our achievement. We were able to turn tragedy into a human triumph, however briefly. In retrospect, this seemed to me a metaphor for life in general.

A judge wrote a "constitution." The chief physician of a major hospital succeeded in preventing epidemics without hospital beds and adequate medication. A restaurateur made our meals as nourishing and tasty as they could be with the measly food supplies we received. Actors and singers did their best to cheer us up. Electricians, auto mechanics, carpenters, cobblers, and barbers offered their skills to prepare unskilled intellectuals for "useful" overseas careers.

One episode stands out. It taught me a lesson that all my schooling couldn't teach me. One morning the bus brought a band of gangsters who became known as the "Wolf gang." It was rumored that they had made their living smuggling Egyptian cigarettes and other goods to Vienna on Danube boats. Their acknowledged leader was Heino Wolf, who looked type-cast from Hollywood: crooked nose, boldly protruding underlip, and a battered hat, which he refused to exchange for our berets. He strutted around in demonstrative defiance. Under his chin billowed a red scarf, which looked like the wattles of a turkey.

As soon as the Wolf gang was assigned a dormitory, they elected their trustee to represent them on our camp council. Of course, they elected Heino. I remember our first trustee meeting after his election. Wolf, his hat at a rakish angle, red scarf bulging, greeted us with a "Hey, pals, now we'll get things done for a change. If you want something from the Committee, just tell me. The guys in Brussels are scared stiff of me."

This, we thought, was the finish of our playing at democracy. The next episode in our Merxplas experiment I would not have dared to invent for any of our short stories. But life is a courageous author.

A few days later a truckload arrived from the Committee with exceptionally heavy sacks of flour, potatoes, and onions.

The unloading crew was called. Three of the men lifted a sack with great effort.

"A little heavy for the professors, eh?" Wolf taunted.

"We can do it," one of the men said, bravely.

"Hold it," Wolf stood threatening. Everyone froze wondering what he was up to.

"I have a gold star, too," Wolf said, savoring our consternation. "That's a job for men. Let me handle this."

He marched into the day room where his friends were playing cards. "Let's go, guys," Wolf ordered. "There's some unloading to do."

The men kept playing, cursing. Wolf stood there, quietly, waiting. Then he pounced forward and, with one thrust of the hand, swept the cards off the table. "Get!" he bellowed.

One of the men jumped up and faced him. Wolf grabbed him by his collar and lifted him off the ground. I had never seen anything like this except in Westerns.

The man began to choke and sputter. Wolf set him down again with a bang and jerked his head toward the door. The man went out and the others followed. Wolf also helped with the unloading.

The next installment of the Wolf saga came only two days later. The hungry masses flowed into the dining hall like lava. They struggled for seats near the center, where the soup cauldrons stood, so that they would be first when the kitchen crew ladled out the soup with its customary bits of potatoes. The extra for the day was dried herring.

Someone smacked the herring against the wall. Others followed. "Every day these goddamned herrings!" they shouted. "The store room is full of food! Let's get it!"

A volcano of rage erupted. Bernhard Klein, the keeper of the store room, was rushed. In terror he surrendered the keys. The guard at the door called for reinforcements.

I clearly remember Wolf's reaction, his very words. "You're all a bunch of shitheads," he said, his voice heavy with contempt. He forced his way through the mass of bodies and snatched the keys from the man who had taken them from Klein. When the man resisted, Wolf gave him a chin hook that sent him against the men behind him. Two huskies who attacked Wolf received knock-out blows. The man exuded pure animal energy. The crowd froze.

"Don't be silly, pals," Wolf said in his husky voice. "I'll get you decent food. Cheese and salami. We unloaded it just a few days ago."

He called on two of his friends. They were about to leave the dining hall for the storage room when the camp director with some guards arrived.

"There was a bit of trouble, chief," Wolf told him. "I've taken care of things, don't worry."

The director nodded approval. Then he and the guards left.

We got our cheese and salami. Klein checked the storeroom. Nothing else was missing.

A few days later the trustees met to select the man who would be responsible for order in the camp. Of course, this "Chief of Police" would work under the camp director, but we would have permission to have our own guards.

I sat next to Wolf when Judge Stein asked for nominations. Wolf grinned. He probably thought this playing at democracy was ridiculous.

Neidhart, the union organizer, spoke up. "I nominate Heino," he said. The idea had crossed my mind, too, but I had dismissed it as an ingenious surprise twist for a story, but crazy in real life.

Neidhart addressed Wolf directly. "You are the only one who can keep this crowd under control. You have proved it."

Wolf sat motionless. Only his owl eyes blinked.

"It would be your responsibility to keep order in the camp," Neidhart said. "You accept the job?"

"Sure," Wolf said, fully in control of himself again.

"Any more nominations?" Neidhart asked. Wolf looked around, and even his wattle-scarf looked threatening. No one uttered a sound.

"Nominations closed," Neidhart announced. "All in favor of making Heino Wolf head of our security department?"

The ayes were a bit thin but unanimous.

"Pals," Wolf said, "I thank you. I'll get things done for you."

Later I asked Judge Stein, "Think it'll work?"

"No," Stein said. "But nothing else will either in this crazy world."

The judge, in spite all his experience with the minds of criminals, proved to be as wrong as the rest of us. He was right about one thing: this was a crazy world. Common sense, with all its traditional values, had vanished. Honesty was no longer the best policy. A penny saved was a penny in Hitler's treasury. Father did not know best—my own father thought nothing would happen to innocent people and ended up in a concentration camp.

Heino Wolf, the gangster, made an efficient police chief. As soon as he was given the responsibility to partake in "government," he used his considerable talents to support authority as strongly as he had once fought it. There were many opportunities for him to restore "law and order." He also showed a gentle side I hadn't expected. In the sessions of the trustees, he was the voice of down-to-earth solutions. He became our friend, especially Dr. Bermann's friend.

Our doctor had marriage trouble, as did many of our married colleagues. Brussels was full of temptations for the wives who were left alone there. When we eventually succeeded in persuading the camp director to grant visiting rights to wives once a month, it was too late for the doctor's wife. Karla Bermann was a dark beauty. She was ten years younger than her husband. A young well-to-do Belgian offered her luxuries she had been used to as the wife of a prominent physician. At first, Bermann had even encouraged her contacts with the Belgian because he hoped the young man would use his connections to procure overseas visas for them.

On New Year's Eve some of us were given a two-day pass from the camp to attend a party the Brussels committee had arranged. They hoped to bring some cheer to our dismal situation. Some Belgians were invited, too, including Karla's new friend. When Bermann realized the depth of Karla's involvement, there was an ugly scene and Bermann slapped the young man's face.

The incident was blown out of all proportion. The Belgian press picked it up and made it the slap of the ungrateful refugees in their host country. Dormant anti-Semitism emerged from under the veneer of civilized tolerance. Bermann was arrested, and there was talk of shipping him back to Germany.

The trustees held an emergency meeting. Suggestions ranged from writing letters to the major newspapers to petitions to the Brussels chief of police, even to the King.

"A lot of good that will do," remarked Wolf, his lips curled in a derisive smirk.

"What would you do?" someone challenged.

"Act, not talk," Wolf said. "A hunger strike."

We called a general meeting. The hunger strike was rejected. It would have come too late anyway. We heard that Bermann had been put on a train to Aachen, the German border town.

That very same day, Wolf disappeared from the camp. Two days later he was back again, disheveled and tightlipped. Bermann's assistant, the young doctor Willy Kruger, removed a bullet from Wolf's leg. Wolf remained tightlipped. There were many rumors, but I never found out for sure what had happened.

The incident had serious consequences for Wolf. He was called to the camp director and stripped of his position as chief of police and trustee. The golden star was removed from his hat. The change in the man was amazing. As soon as responsibility was taken from him, he became again the irresponsible head of a brutal gang. He stirred up the unrest that, as a gold-star chief of police, he had kept in check.

Forty years later, when I prepared the final draft of my Merxplas book, I visited the camp with my wife. It still housed vagrants picked from the streets and slums. But everything else had changed. The massive red brick buildings were whitewashed in antiseptic uniformity. In the dormitories forty beds were still lined up like piano keys, but each bed had a night stand and a small chest of drawers. Each dorm had a sink with running water. The dorms had central heating, as had the day room and the library. Indoor flush toilets had replaced the outdoor stinkholes. A little room, smelling of medicines, had been set aside for the sick. The room was empty at the time. I sat down on one of the beds. It seemed to me that Dr. Bermann sat next to me.

"How I fought for a room like this!" he says. "And for a closet full of medicines! We didn't even have running water to clean wounds. We had to go to the kitchen for a pailfull."

I am not so much interested in old gripes but want to clear up some loose ends. "What happened at that time in Aachen?" I ask. I had often speculated about this.

"You won't believe this," I make Berman say. "I didn't believe it myself. I was holed up in this Aachen prison cell, you know, with SS guards standing outside. All signs told me that I was going to be shipped back to Germany.

"On the second morning the steel door opened. A Nazi guard motioned me to come with him. There was Heino in the waiting room, very matter-of-fact, you know how he was, no big deal. He told me later the guard was a friend of his. I guess all those smugglers and gangsters stick to each other. That Nazi guards were gangsters was no surprise. Anyway, Heino didn't explain much and hustled me along. His plan was to get me across the Dutch border. I couldn't go back to Belgium.

"Crossing into Holland was the dangerous part. You have heard a lot of stories of refugees being smuggled through forests and across rivers, running from border police. We did all that. We were shot at, and Heino was hurt. He just bandaged his wound with a piece of his underwear. He didn't even ask my help.

"He had a friend in a village just across the Dutch border, and he left me with his friend. I asked him why he didn't stay. He just said he had some business to attend to. You know, I had other indications before that Heino and his gang had ulterior motives for staying in the camp. He had underground connections everywhere. He could have hidden with them. But Heino and his gang let themselves be interned. Maybe they were waiting for some smuggled goods to come in, perhaps on a ship, and they used Merxplas as a safe place to hide. Anyway, I'll be grateful to him forever; he saved my life.

"And another thing, Wolf told Karla where I was and told his Dutch friend to get her to me. He had a fist of iron and a heart of gold. You know, gangsters stick to their friends, and I was his friend. I called him 'gold-star Heino.' That gold star meant so much to him. Life kicked him around a lot, and he kicked back. Then we made him chief of police. Heino Wolf, the gangster, chief of police! With a gold star!"

Here I was sitting in Merxplas again. I poured all the anxieties and hopes of my past forty years into this imaginary figure next to me, and made him say what I wanted so badly to hear. There were so many unanswered questions, so many uncertain, probably unhappy, endings! I made Dr. Bermann make everything come out all right.

"When the Nazis overran Holland, I joined the underground. They needed a doctor. Karla was my nurse. Heino's friend had brought her back to me. We were as close as ever. Her Brussels episode was forgiven and forgotten. When the war ended, we returned to Vienna and I became a staff member of the General Hospital. I am now the head of its department of internal medicine."

"You know anything about the others?"

"I have kept in touch with my 'staff' at Merxplas. My assistant, Dr. Kruger, has a practice in New York. Kurt Berber, the ballet dancer who

helped as a nurse, is with a dancing company in Sao Paolo. Klimt, the pharmacist, has his own pharmacy in Brisbane, Australia. Fritz Gruber, the medical student, finished his studies in Toronto and is practicing there. They are all safe."

Reality was more murderous. I have found only one of my fellow Merxplas refugees.

It now seems difficult to believe that I spent only four months in Merxplas. It was one of the most formative and instructive times of my life. For the first time I saw humans in their raw diversity—their egocentricities, their fears, their jungle instincts for survival. But I also saw their capacity to care, to hope, to help, to comfort, to plan, to respond to challenges, and to work toward goals, even if those goals were distant and uncertain. We were victimized but we refused to be victims.

I didn't see all this until I was in control of my life again in the security of America. In my refugee period I had been as egocentric in my attempts to crawl out of my own hole as the rest. I was just luckier. And it took a number of miracles. Not supernatural miracles with thunder and lightning and messages from above, but miracles nevertheless, disguised as coincidences.

In Vienna, I had stood in line with hundreds of others at the American embassy hoping to acquire a low quota number. The United States permitted only a certain number of immigrants from a specific country every year. The annual quota number for Austrians was six thousand, sufficient for normal times but below the needs of the tens of thousands who wanted to flee to America in 1938.

The quota for that year soon was filled and the rest of us hoped for a number low enough to qualify for 1939. A low quota number, however, was not the only precondition for entry into the Promised Land. In addition, an affidavit from an American citizen was required, one who was wealthy enough to guarantee that the immigrant would not become a financial burden to the country. Not many refugees were able to find such a sponsor, and those who didn't lost their place in the quota system.

Although I finally got my number, I had no affidavit and no realistic hope of getting one. It was Max in London who tried to create the next miracle for me. He went to the London public library and picked out some namesakes of mine from the Hollywood phone book because he figured that Hollywood would be the most promising place for an aspiring writer.

An Oxford student, the translator of our short stories, drafted a letter in excellent English describing my plight and hopes. While still in Vienna, I wrote letters to about a dozen Epsteins in Hollywood. We saw Hollywood as a paradise for writers. It had been a ray of hope during my stay in the Brussels prison when a letter from my parents informed me that I had received a nibble from a banker in Hollywood who asked for more information.

I asked the elderly businessman who taught our first English class to give the required information to my putative sponsor. I never heard from my Hollywood Epstein. Two years later, when I was a California resident myself, I contacted him. He told me that the letter I had sent him from Merxplas had been in such poor English that he had considered me a phony.

After my attempt to find a Hollywood sponsor ended in failure, I experienced another miracle, or rather a string of miracles. My father had a slight acquaintance with one person in America, Martin Becker, who had been an employee at the municipal storehouse where my father worked. Becker had gone to America in the early thirties when immigration was still easy. Father now wrote a letter asking Becker if he could send an affidavit for me. Becker replied that the immigration authorities had informed him that his financial resources were not strong enough to become a sponsor.

Meanwhile father had been told by a distant relative in Prague that, in the 1880s, one of my grandfather's cousins had emigrated to the United States under circumstances that were hushed up by the family. This man, Karl Beck, had been considered a black sheep and the family had long lost contact with him. Father wrote to Becker asking him to find this Karl Beck, a preposterous request, as I realize now. Father did not know that residents are not registered in America as they are in Europe.

Mr. Becker was a practical man. He lived in Trenton, New Jersey, and the first thing he did was look in the Trenton phone book. He found a Charles Beck who was not the man Becker was searching for. But Charles Beck had heard about a namesake who lived in nearby South Orange. Another look in a phone book, this time of South Orange, got Becker in touch with Sophie, the widow of our long-lost Karl (Americanized to Charles) Beck. Sophie was sympathetic to the plight of the far-away Epstein clan and sent an affidavit for me to the Belgian consul. Father had assured her that the sponsorship would only be a formality and that I was a published writer and Doctor of Law who would be able to support himself.

And so, out of the blue, I received notification in Merxplas to come to the American consulate in Antwerp for an interview. The news electrified not only me but all the inmates who possessed those precious quota numbers. There certainly was envy, even among my friends, but also hope.

This auspicious beginning ended in disastrous disappointment. Every American consul had the right to set his own conditions to make sure a new immigrant would not become a financial burden to the United States, which still suffered from the Great Depression. Rumors had it that the Consul in Antwerp was especially strict. Neither I nor anyone else in the camp was prepared for the extra condition the Consul demanded of me: a locked account of $3,000 in an American bank from which only $50 a month could be withdrawn. Neither I nor any other of the prospective immigrants could hope to meet such a demand. All we had been allowed to take with us from Germany were ten marks.

My story cast a spell of gloom over the camp. But again, Max's ingenuity found a way out for me. A law had recently been passed in England that allowed a refugee who had a quota number and an affidavit to await the maturing of the number in England. A refugee had to possess one hundred English pounds and promise not to seek employment while in England.

I had been told at the Consulate that my quota number would not come up for another year. The one hundred pounds were within reach from the royalties from our stories that Max had sold in England. I had been busy writing in my prison cell and in Merxplas—whenever and wherever I could find a quiet corner in this anthill of humanity. The rest of the required amount would come from the sale of a clump of gold (mostly from my melted tooth fillings) I had smuggled out.

The American Ambassador in London was known to set no extra conditions for immigration. And I would be free again, living with Max and his parents, whom he had been able to rescue from Vienna. (Another miracle: the family of Max's mother was very distantly related to the Rothschilds and Max, in his incredible inventiveness, had managed to wangle a two-minute interview with Lionel de Rothschild, who agreed to support his parents' request for immigration.)

So in March of 1939, I said an emotional good-bye to those I was leaving behind in Merxplas. There was a drop of sadness in my happiness of having a future again, uncertain as it was. I realized, even then, that here an important phase of my life had come to an end and that these four months would have a lasting impact.

The parting from that little group, who had set up a quixotic republic in a camp for vagabonds, was especially painful. We had struggled toward a common goal, and I felt closer to them than to many other people I got to know in later years. This episode showed me that periods which are important in shaping our lives are not necessarily happy times but most often times of struggle and despair, times that make sense only in retrospect.

The remarkable thing about my year in England is that I remember so little of it. It was not a painful year that had to be banished into the dungeons of my unconscious. It was a hiatus between the miseries of the last year and anxiety about the next.

It was, in fact, a time of recovery. I had acquired an ulcer in Merxplas and received tender loving care from Max's mother, who cooked a special milk diet for me. Max and I shared a room and could discuss story ideas without walking to each other's homes, as we had done in Vienna. And I acquired an English girlfriend, Grace, who was my comforter, lover, and English teacher.

Refugee boys, especially those from Vienna, were much in demand. English girls were charmed by our customs of hand kissing, adjusting chairs for them, and holding doors open.

Clubs were formed to invite us for dinner, hikes, barbecues, dances, and parties. Grace was a telephone operator and had clear diction, which was a great help for my learning the complexities of English pronunciation. She was an ideal partner, but even of her I have only a fragmented recollection.

What I repressed most was my year-long struggle to enable my parents to join me in America. It was clear that staying in Vienna held mortal danger. Our angel, Sophie Beck, had sent them affidavits but their quota numbers were high because they had not registered early enough. In addition, there was one obstacle after another—exit permits, passports, tax clearance, and other chicaneries the Nazis were so good at thinking up. Money for ship tickets had to be raised. Tickets were not issued until the visa was imminent. The visas were not issued until the quota number was close to maturity. War broke out in Europe in September 1939. Although this did not prevent immigration to the United States, it made stopovers in European countries like England no longer viable.

The morning after the declaration of war is one of the few moments I remember clearly. It was one of those times in my odyssey when I felt split in two, as I did when I pounded my fist against the steel door of my cell in the Brussels prison. One half of me was terrified by the actual situation, and the other half saw the possibilities of a story in the making. We had been issued gas masks and informed of the location of the nearest air-raid shelter. On that cold September morning, the warning sirens began screeching, and we all—Max, his parents, and I—jumped out of bed, put on our masks and, still in our pajamas, ran for our designated shelter. Dozens of people ran in all directions in the same pajama-gas-mask costume. We all were terrified. I saw the humor of the situation only in the safety of later days.

The siren turned out to be a false alarm. We returned to the normalcy of the apartment. But life was far from normal. Max worked for the *Jewish Chronicle.* He found an opportunity to use his knowledge of German for an English paper. He even received government permission to accept employment because—as the *Chronicle* claimed—he was especially qualified. It was his job to scan German papers for items of interest to English Jewish readers.

After war broke out, the staff of the *Chronicle* was evacuated to High Wycomb, and we all moved—Max, his parents, and I. Here we lived in heavenly peace, but I felt restless because I saw no purpose. I could not promote my further emigration nor that of my parents. In addition, the world seemed at peace when I knew it was a slaughterhouse.

The absurdity of our situation was illustrated by the following incident. Our village neighbors were more concerned with their garden clubs and tea parties than with the threat that had befallen Europe. One lady invited us for tea. Max and I tried to tell her of the Nazi threat. She led us to her rose garden and confronted us with an argument she considered unassailable. With a sweeping gesture toward her prize roses, she called out, "You mean to say that Hitler will come and destroy all *this*?"

In February 1940, I received the long-awaited note from the American Embassy in London. My quota number had matured, and I could pick up my visa. Except for a few formalities with the High Wycomb police force (all Jewish refugees from Germany and Austria had been classified as "enemy aliens" and needed permission to travel to London), I encountered no more difficulties.

Saying good-bye to Max was almost as heartbreaking as my good-byes to my parents. We didn't know whether we would ever see each other again. But even miracles that seem to be coincidences need our help and preparation, our planning and foresight. Although Max didn't believe in "God," he kept helping God to perform miracles. Max had prepared his flight from Austria, had helped me get to England and eventually to the United States, and he performed miracles in repeatedly finding jobs for himself and for me. Yet, in one important instance he failed. He failed to foresee the necessity that eventually he, too, would have to find refuge in America. He had fled to London immediately and felt safe there. He did not take the precaution of getting an American quota number.

The difference of our world views came to the fore. Max feared the worst—a Nazi invasion of England. The German troops were poised in France at the English channel. I faced the uncertainties of my future with apprehension but also with hopeful curiosity. I looked forward to the surprise endings life would have in store for me. And I had the conviction, based on nothing, that these surprises endings would be happy ones.

The American Way of Life

In Vienna we had seen America as the land of golden opportunities, and my first experience seemed to confirm this. After a seventeen-day trip across the Atlantic in a slow convoy, our ship landed in Boston. It was early morning. Coffee and pancakes had been prepared in a large warehouse by ladies of all ages who engaged us in cheerful conversations. The woman who sat down next to me was about my age, beautifully dressed, and curious "to know all about Hitler." When she heard my story and that my sponsor lived in New Jersey, she asked me if I wanted to stay with her family for a couple of days to "catch my breath."

The name of my welcoming angel was Gladys Bankman. She drove me in her shiny car to a house in the suburbs. Her house had a snow-covered front lawn, a play yard in back, and a double garage. Every room had furniture that looked as if it had been bought yesterday. Two children's rooms were full of toys. The kitchen and the utility room sparkled with appliances I recognized from American movies. Gladys showed me "the" guest room, with its own bathroom.

The children came home from school. I was introduced as "our visitor from Vienna," and we all had ice cream. When I went to my room to freshen up, I was convinced that this rich family would help me get on my feet. Mr. Bankman presumably was one of those famous American millionaires with connections, perhaps even in the newspaper world. I was looking forward to meeting him.

I met Mr. Bankman, a friendly and quiet man, at the dinner table. I was convinced that he was an important man in an important position. After the children went to bed, I told the Bankmans of my hopes to establish myself as a writer in America. Gladys assured me I would be successful.

Before falling asleep that night, I had a short happy ending fantasy.

Mr. Bankman takes me to the bank where he is director. He introduces me to a business friend who knows Mr. Epstein in Hollywood, the one who had offered me an affidavit but had not replied to my last letter. We phone Epstein. He apologizes—he had misplaced my letter. He knows several movie producers and wants me to come to Hollywood to meet them.

I go to New York, sell several of my translated short stories. When I have enough money, I take a train to California. Mr. Epstein introduces me to Mr. Preminger, who had been the director of the Kammerspiele Theater in Vienna and now is directing movies in Hollywood. Mr. Preminger offers me a contract and gives me a translator. I am on my way.

Again, reality turned out to be quite different. When I came down to breakfast the next morning, the children were already eating, while Gladys scrambled eggs for her husband. When he joined us, I swallowed my surprise. He wore overalls and carried a hard hat and a lunch pail. He ate hurriedly, kissed Gladys good-bye, and left.

I burst out; "Your husband is a laborer?"

She nodded cheerfully, not noticing my European class prejudice. "He works in a Ford factory," she said proudly. This was my first lesson of the American way of life.

Others followed soon enough. The bus trip to New York and the rent for the first week, in a little cubby hole in a rabbit warren where I shared facilities with other refugees, used up almost all of my dollar reserves. I got in touch with Sophie Beck's daughter Blanche, who worked as a secretary on Wall Street. She took me to South Orange to meet her mother, my sponsor, a sweet old lady, who had little understanding for my ambition to make a living as a writer. She gave me a twenty-dollar bill which, with the few dollars I still had, was enough for three weeks of rent. The American way of life, she indicated, was to start from scratch with "real" work. All her three boys, she said proudly, had started as newspaper boys and baggers in grocery stores.

But even these jobs were not available in this time of depression. The other refugees in my rabbit warren were desperately looking for jobs, any jobs. One of them, an engineer, had found work in a slaughterhouse, holding chickens while they were getting shots. Another one, a successful playwright, carried ice blocks from the basement to the third floor of a brothel.

Still, I believed that our Peter Fabrizius stories, which had been published in many countries in Europe, would also sell in America. I went from one editorial office to the other. I never got further than the receptionist. In Vienna I had talked directly to the editor, or at least to his secretary. At the end of the second week I seemed to get the break I was hoping for. I discovered a new weekly called *Friday* on the racks of a drug store. The editor not only talked to me but showed interest in the documents of my emigration. He bought the rights to use these documents in a story he would write. He also bought one of our spy stories. He paid $120 which financed my meager living expenses for another few weeks. I continued my search for similarly sympathetic editors, but in vain.

I looked forward to the publication of the two stories with great anticipation. They appeared on two consecutive Fridays. I was in shock. The story of my emigration hardly mentioned the many chicaneries of the Nazis and overemphasized the restrictions by the British—the travel ban, the police registrations, our classification as "enemy aliens." Our spy story was given a new surprise ending that showed the British in a treacherous light. This was particularly upsetting because Britain had been the only country kind enough to allow me to await the maturing of my American quota number. Why would an American magazine paint them in such a bad light?

The playwright who carried ice blocks in the brothel knew the answer. *Friday* magazine was a new publication of the Communist Party of America. It followed the party line of the Soviet-Nazi pact. The Nazis were now Soviet allies, and the British were the enemy. This disclosure cut off my only source of income as a writer. I was warned not to affiliate myself with a Communist publication.

When my money ran out I had to join my fellow refugees in looking for a job. From what I could see, this was a pretty hopeless undertaking. Max, who was so good in sniffing out job opportunities, was in England trying to get out before a feared Nazi invasion.

Willy Beer, the distant relative who had supplied us with the material for our first Peter Fabrizius story about the Indians as oil millionaires, had opened a small ski-binding factory in New York. He offered me a job for $12 a week. He warned me that it would be hard work on a dye-pressing machine. It was hard work. But everyone in my rabbit warren envied me. I had started my American way of life. From rags to riches. I had arrived at the rags.

But I was happy. I had met my life mate-to-be, and she introduced me to some of her relatives and friends. I had sprouted some tiny rootlets in the Promised Land.

I met Judith in 1940, shortly after my arrival in New York. She had lost her parents and lived in a home for working girls, the Clara de Hirsch Residence. Many refugees from Europe also lived there, including Jeannette, who was engaged to a writer I knew from Vienna. When Jeannette met me, she told me half-kiddingly that a twenty-eight-year-old bachelor like me should not go to waste when fifty girls at the Clara de Hirsch were looking for husbands. She selected Judith as the top candidate. It was a lucky choice. Judith and I met September 2. We married two months later. I now can identify many of the rungs that enabled me to climb back out of the abyss of self-disdain. The strongest was Judith's unhesitating decision to marry this penniless refugee.

Was it love at first sight? We thought so, but looking back with the wisdom of hindsight, I know it was loneliness, an emotional void, and physical attraction which first manifested itself when we danced together. There were also practical considerations, at least on my part. Judith was born in New York from Austrian parents. She spoke English and German and could type and take shorthand in both languages. She was the ideal partner for teaching me to speak and write in English, for translating my old short stories, and for typing the new ones. The practical considerations on her part are less clear to me. I was a doctor of laws that weren't even valid in my own country any more, and a writer in a language that was useless in America. She married me not for what I was but for the potentialities she saw, which I myself could not see and which she helped me develop.

Our wedding was the simplest affair possible. We married in the home of a rabbi, himself a refugee from the Nazis. We walked into his dining room under the traditional Jewish canopy, the *chuppah,* held up by four posts carried by Judith's boss, a cousin, Sofie Beck's daughter Blanche, and my schoolmate Harry Freud. Harry, with the typical humor of the Freud family, whispered to me while we marched in ceremoniously, "A wedding where I hold up the *chuppah* cannot end well." Fortunately, after fifty-seven years, I know he was wrong.

Harry was one of the few refugees whose family had money in America. He owned a car. So he drove us from the wedding to a bed-and-breakfast place in New Jersey. We finished our honeymoon the next morning by walking back to Manhattan over the George Washington Bridge. How I wished my parents could have been with me at the ceremony! But, in a way, they were. Unbeknownst to all but me, they marched with us into the tiny dining room of the rabbi.

"How will it all end?" Mother says fearfully. "Bubi earns $12 a week as a factory worker."

"Judith earns another $12 as a secretary," Father comforts her. "Besides Bubi went to Willy, who gave him his job. When Bubi told him he was getting married, Willy gave Bubi a raise. Bubi now earns $13 a week."

"Thirteen," Mother sighs. She has always been superstitious and sees the number as a bad omen. "How will it all come out? Bubi cannot make a living by writing, as he wants, because he doesn't know the language. And what he knows about Austrian laws does him no good. He cannot be a factory worker forever."

"Judith is an American," Father tells her. "She knows English and German. She is a secretary. She even knows English and German shorthand. She'll help him. America is the land of opportunities. He'll make his way."

"I know he will," Mother agrees. "But I can't help worrying. And we can't do anything for him."

"He is no longer a child, Irma. He will make his way," Father tells her.

"We have always helped him when he was in trouble," Mother says. "Now we can't do anything."

"Maybe later we can. He's trying to get us to America. I'll get a job. You can get a job too. It's not hard for even an elderly woman to get a job as a cook or a housekeeper. In fact, it's easier for women to get a job than for men."

"You have always been an optimist, Ernstl. What can we do? We lost everything and he has nothing."

"I'll think of something."

"Yes, you were always good at finding ways. But this time it's different, harder than ever. Oh, Ernstl," she sighs, "do you think we have brought him up so he will be able to live in this terrible world? Maybe we have spoiled him too much."

"No, Irma, we gave him our love. That's the most valuable gift. Now he has Judith. She will continue what we started. She is a good woman, a little bit like you. She believes in him. Just as we did. Trust me."

"I always did. But things are different. Everything is different, much harder. Times have changed."

"But he hasn't," Father says firmly. "There's something that remains firm in us, regardless of what happens."

I listen to them while we walk under the wedding canopy. I don't know what that something is that is so firm and unchangeable, but I know that father is right, against all evidence. He's always been right.

We come to the rabbi and for a moment I have the unreal feeling that I have melted with Father and Judith with Mother. And from the distance I hear myself say, "I do."

After the wedding, Judith's friends in the Clara de Hirsch Residence gave us a wedding party. We received two wedding gifts—a collapsible bridge table and four matching chairs from Sophie Beck and a radio from Judith's employer. We had found a furnished room in the home of another refugee family, who gave us room and board for $20 a week, so we had $5 of spending money each week. We moved in, bringing along our wedding gifts.

In the Spring the ski season ended, and I learned another lesson about the American Way. Willy Beer closed shop and from one day to the next I was out of a job. I had no funds. Judith had just enough to last us two weeks. I tried to find a job, any job, but New York was overrun with job seekers. So we moved to a farm in North Grosvenordale, Connecticut, owned by friends of Judith's family. Judith's family had spent many summer vacations and Christmases at the farm.

It was a primitive farm, with no electricity or running water. To get water we had to pump an outside well. One day I pumped up a frog. Mrs. Einsle, the farmer's wife, told me frogs keep the water clean. Judith and I found this romantic. It fitted our honeymoon mood.

The best thing about the little town of North Grosvenordale was that the cotton mill needed workers. The mill was two miles away. A neighbor who worked there took me to and from the mill. It was a back-breaking job, literally, and I still have a sore back more than fifty years later. It was my job to take the empty bobbins, which are about ten feet long, on a dolly to the cotton-spinning machine and to take the loaded bobbins back to the warehouse. I hadn't known that people could handle such weights, but I was glad to have the job. In my mind I showed my hands with their forming calluses to Gretl and the spitting Nazi. "See—I can do it! I can work with my hands!"

My weekly salary was now $18. I was on my way up!

Meanwhile Max had fled to a ghetto in the Japanese-occupied Shanghai. Shanghai was the only place on earth that required no visa. Max had feared a Nazi invasion of England. In a panic, he had found a rare boat to Shanghai, which was overrun by desperate refugees. This gave me the opportunity to repay my debt to him for saving me from Merxplas. I was able to persuade three people to scrape together enough guarantee money to make out an affidavit—a very hesitant relative of Max, a refugee friend of his family, and my good schoolmate Harry Freud. Max arrived in San Francisco in July 1941, just five months before Pearl Harbor, which would have made any travel from the Far East impossible.

I often thought about whether it's better to be a pessimist like Max, foresee dangers, and escape in time, or an optimist like myself, who trusts that things, with the help of miracles, will somehow turn out all right. The experiment was inconclusive. In Vienna, Max had correctly foreseen the Nazi invasion of Austria and had prepared for his (and eventually my) escape. I naively had hoped nothing would happen, and got caught. A year later Max had erred in pessimistically expecting a Nazi invasion of England and fled to Shanghai, where he could have been trapped, while I had trusted fate and, with a little help on my part and all those miracles, had made it to America.

Once Max arrived in San Francisco, there was no question that we should get together again. We were in the same country, only three thousand miles apart. The question was whether Judith and I should join him in San Francisco, or he should come to New York. Fortunately we decided to go West. There was a place on Broadway that arranged shared car rides for people travelling all over the country. Two Berkeley students drove us from the East Coast to the West Coast for $23 each.

Our possessions, two suitcases, the table-set, the radio, and my portable typewriter, filled the space between front- and backseats and served as our bed while our two students drove continuously for three days and nights.

Max had again shown his ingenuity by digging up livelihoods for all three of us. He managed to get a job in Berkeley as tutor for the two boys of C.S. Forester, author of the Captain Hornblower books. Max persuaded Mrs. Forester to let Judith and me have the garden cottage in exchange for my working in the garden and Judith in the house. In addition I found a job cleaning toilets and ashtrays in a university fraternity house. Again I thought with satisfaction of Gretl and the spitting Nazi.

When America joined the war in December 1941, my optimism again got the best of me. It was the first gleam of hope that the seemingly invincible German army machine could be stopped. I still had the illusion, which I shared with so many refugees, that things would return to normal and that I could go back and pick up the pieces where my life had been interrupted.

We lived in an unreal world. Berkeley was as peaceful as ever. The papers, the newsreels, and the radio reported the fighting and violence. Also Pearl Harbor had cut off all immigration to the United States.

My parents already had their visa and ship tickets. For a while there was a flicker of hope of getting them to Cuba, but the ship tickets had to be transferred and ships to Cuba were overcrowded and tickets unavailable. Communication with my parents was restricted to twenty-five-word Red Cross messages, which took three months to arrive. I got one such message and I sent one—that Judith was carrying their grandchild. I hope they received the news, although I doubt if they would have been overly cheered. Father was too logical and mother too superstitious to welcome the idea of bringing children into this world.

Then silence. I did not know it then—the "final solution" had begun.

The entry of the United States in the war against the Nazis gave life purpose again. Max and I went to work in the Richmond shipyard, my next small step toward riches—$62 for a forty-eight-hour week. It was exhausting work. We both had been rejected by the draft board because of near-sightedness. Mass-producing Liberty ships let us do our little share to defeat Hitler.

All of a sudden America had become a seller's market for jobseekers. When I applied at the hiring office, the girl behind the desk asked me what job I wanted.

"I want to build a ship," I told her.

"I know," she said. "But there are sixty kinds of jobs. Right now they need shipfitters."

I wanted to know what shipfitters do.

"Beats me," she said. "Report to work tomorrow at eight and they'll tell you."

Max and I were both assigned to the crew on Assembly Way Five, where pre-assembled parts of the 10,500-ton Liberty ship were waiting to be put together. The pre-assembled pieces were lifted by cranes to the hull and welded in place.

We were among the first in this new ship-building venture. When I reported to work, the men of my assembly crew, including the leaderman and the foreman, did not know much more about ship building than I did.

On that first day I saw a group of men crowding around a blueprint. According to these plans, our crew was supposed to assemble some bulkheads. I joined the back of the group but didn't understand why they were cursing and scratching their heads. My English still was weak, and they spoke in various accents, from New England to Texas.

The more I listened the more it became clear to me that I knew the answer to what puzzled them. When there was a moment of silence, I timidly said, "I think the dotted line means the bracket goes on the other side." Everybody turned to look at the greenhorn with the heavy accent.

"Can you read a blueprint?" the leaderman asked.

"I learned how in high school," I answered, modestly.

They drew me into their inner circle. We spent the rest of the day going through the blueprints of all the parts our crew was going to assemble. Of course, my time of glory didn't last long because once they understood the blueprints of the few bulkheads we built over and over again, they didn't need me any more. But that one day gave me an unbelievable boost. After a long time, I had again been Someone and Useful.

Gretl prepared the soil for the Nazis who considered me, as all Jews, as useless insects that needed to be exterminated. This image of myself was reinforced by that incident of my cleaning the sidewalk and being spit upon in the face. At that time I already had a Doctor's degree in Law, was a successful short story writer, and had girlfriends, but I was still vulnerable to Gretl's disdain and the Nazi atmosphere of humiliation.

Looking back on those incidents, I realize that beneath all the self-doubt, deep within me, was a healthy core, a spark that waited to be lit. During my years of emigration, Gretl and the spitting Nazi with the worker's callused hands who scorned my soft ones, became constant challengers. Whenever I accomplished something I considered a success—the backbreaking work in a cotton mill in Connecticut, the cleaning of ashtrays and toilets as janitor in Berkeley, the forty-eight-hour-a-week labor in the shipyards of Richmond—I saw Gretl's mocking face and the Nazi's devastating grimace, and I told them, "See? I did it! I survived!"

Our gang consisted of about two dozen men and women, many of whose real names I never really knew. We called each other by nicknames painted on our steel helmets. There was Jason, a rancher from Montana; Pee-Wee, a housewife from Connecticut whose husband had been drafted; Alibi, a miner from Minnesota; Pink, a college student from Berkeley; and Gosh, an old shipfitter from Maine; the only member of the gang who had ever built a ship. He was so puzzled by the new methods that he constantly shook his head and mumbled "Gosh!" in wonderment. There was Red, a laundry man from Oklahoma; Lovella, a waitress from Utah; Ma Hopkins, a grandmother from southern California; Happy, a railway cook from South Carolina; Dimples, a movie starlet from Washington; and Swede, a disabled war veteran from Arkansas.

This was the staff of my graduate school in English. I learned that "get off your filthy dime" meant I should hurry up. When someone asked me, "Would you like to give me a hand?" it was not a polite question but an order. I took notes of all those phrases, spoken in Texas, New England, and Arkansas accents. These notes came in handy later when I wrote stories in English.

This was the time when all hopes for my parents' emigration ended, and also the time when we could afford to have our first child, Wendy. My sense of responsibleness received a strong boost the day Wendy was born. When I first saw this red-faced, wrinkled bundle through the window pane in the maternity ward, her eyes were closed. Then one of them opened and looked straight at me. I realized that from now on I was responsible for a human being. The old generation in

Europe had perished, and we were starting to build a new one in America.

During my shipyard years I changed from emigrant to immigrant, from refugee to citizen. I was content building these ships, so vital for the war. During the three years I worked there, the average time for building a Liberty ship was cut from 241 to 28 days and, as a stunt, the Robert E. Perry was assembled in 4½ days. But Max was restless. He wanted us to go back to a writing career and found a way to do it, even though our English was less than perfect. The Office of War Information in San Francisco had begun its short-wave broadcasts to the Far East. Max managed to convince the head of the China Department that two Austrians were suited to report the war in Europe to the Chinese.

This was not as absurd as it sounds. We knew the geography of Europe, so we knew the places where battles were fought and bombs were dropped. Our deficiencies in English did not matter, Max argued, because our reports had to be translated into Cantonese and Mandarin. It made no difference when we sometimes used a wrong preposition or an awkward English phrase.

We were still writing short-wave broadcasts to the Chinese when the war ended. All activities of the Office of War Information were concentrated in New York, and the office was renamed Voice of America. Some of the San Francisco staff members were given a chance to transfer to the New York office. Judith was homesick for New York, while Charlotte, Max's wife, had a good position as secretary to the President of the University of California at Berkeley and didn't want to move.

So we decided for the first and only time to part ways by our own volition. We established our feature agency, Pacific Features, for the newly opened European markets. I was to find outlets on the East Coast. Factual reports were easier to sell than fiction, especially to trade magazines.

In New York, I worked for the English section of the Voice of America. My reports, mostly about cultural events and editorial round-ups, no longer were translated but used as I wrote them. My schooling in the English language was now complete, thanks to my teachers—Grace in London, Judith in New York, the shipyard workers in Richmond, and our colleagues in the Chinese Department of the Office of War Information in San Francisco. Now I was in my final graduate class—the Voice of America in New York. I have never lost my Austrian accent, but it didn't show in my writing.

The Religious Search

The war was over. Millions had been killed—on battlefields, in concentration camps, in their homes, on the ground, in the air, at sea. Other millions had been maimed, starved, orphaned, and widowed. The deaths of my parents in all their excruciating details were confirmed by two survivors. Although I tried for years to bring them to America, they were deported to the Theresienstadt concentration camp in 1942. My father was taken from a hospital to be loaded into a cattle wagon. My mother, who was not yet on the transport list, insisted on going with him. He barely survived the trip and died soon after arrival. Two survivors, distant relatives, told me that they saw my mother near death in Theresienstadt. She was withdrawn and had lost her will to live. She literally died of a broken heart.

As an adult, nothing has burdened me more than my failure to save my parents from the concentration camps. I took this as a responsibleness I failed to fulfill. This was an unhappy ending I had to accept, and it produced a heavy burden of guilt. Most of my family had vanished. The rest were struggling in various parts of the world to rebuild their lives. What kind of a world was this? What kind of God would allow such evil to triumph for so long? Hitler had been defeated, not as a punishment for being evil but because he had met superior forces of strength. Power, not morality, ruled the world.

I had survived, but better men and women than I had perished. I could see no justice, only luck and chance. I recalled a furious attack I had made on the columns of ants when they marched through my prison cell in Brussels, following their leader blindly like Nazi columns. I had pounced on them in frustration and trampled them to death by the hundreds, but there were always survivors. They hobbled away on four or five of their six legs, having survived in a little groove in the floor or in a dimple of my shoe sole.

Was this how God operated? Did our survival depend on our happening to find shelter in a dimple in God's sole when he pounced on us? Where was the God of love which was praised by all major religions? What I saw was a God of indifference at best, a God of vengeance at worst. But vengeance for what? My parents had never done any harm to anybody. This was either an arbitrary God, or there was no God at all.

I could accept neither outlook. I was searching for a God concept that made sense to me within my own experiences. A personal God who looked the other way, like my schoolmates had done, while millions were tortured and killed was unacceptable to my mind and heart. But the cynical view that "God played dice" with us and that everything was chance and whim was equally intolerable. I wanted to believe in a God who created and maintained a world that made sense, in spite of all the obvious nonsense, chaos, and injustice.

The Holocaust has turned some of my friends into cynical nonbelievers who cannot accept the existence of a God who could allow such a wholesale slaughter of innocents. Others have become more fervently religious, clinging to a God who moves in mysterious ways and always for our good even if we cannot understand.

I remembered the words of a little girl, long, long ago, in Vienna. It is strange how often little children say something that sounds simple, even banal, and we laugh about it, and later we recognize it as a piece of wisdom. This little girl had recovered from the measles, and her father told her, "See, God made you well again." And she replied, "Yes, Papa, but why did he made me sick in the first place?"

Recalling these words in Berkeley twenty years later, they seemed to raise a crucial question. Here I was the survivor. I had survived through a string of miracles. I was safe in America. I had started a new career at a great university. I was united again with Max. I had found a wonderful helpmate and had started to build a new family. Thank you, God, and a thousand times thank you, God. But why had God allowed the Holocaust in the first place?

This was when my religious search began in earnest. I called it my "reality search for God." I didn't mean it irreverently, I simply wanted to make my best possible effort to find out what Divinity really, really might be like, how it worked, and how I could relate to it.

I know that millions of people have found a great variety of answers that satisfy them. The answers were given to them by tradition, upbringing, and their churches or synagogues. I know that they feel secure in their beliefs. I envied them, but their beliefs were not the answers I sought. I was convinced that my faith could not be dictated; it must grow from the inside of me, from my personal experiences. And the faith given by established religions did not check with my experiences.

When I say today that I have found an answer, at least to my satisfaction and peace of mind, I strongly suspect that this was possible not in spite of but because of my experiences of suffering. I would not wish these experiences on my worst enemy, but once they did happen to me and had become an unalterable part of my life, they became a source of strength and growth. This is true, I believe, of any kind of unavoidable suffering. It is, of course, not necessary to go through a holocaust to learn the lessons of life. There are many kinds and degrees of suffering. What is bearable to one person is agony to another. But I have become convinced that all suffering carries the seeds of growth.

The miseries of my teens, my self-doubts and anxieties, were no less a burden to me than my later experiences in jail, Merxplas, back-breaking labor, and the frustrating struggle to save my parents. Actually, I had a greater fear of the future as a teen-ager than as a refugee. Once I had become successful as a lover, writer, and friend, I had little doubt that I would also be successful as a survivor. This was an early manifestation of faith, although I did not give it that religious-sounding name. It was a hope based, not on outside facts, but on my inner optimistic attitude.

I certainly had my share of unavoidable and meaningless suffering. Looking back, I can see that meaning—important meaning—has emerged from it. Not that the Holocaust retroactively acquired meaning. No, it was and remains evil and meaningless. Meaning emerged through the way I looked at my painful experiences. They made me see that it mattered less what actually happened to me, and more how I took it—as a defeat or a challenge.

Nietzsche said, "When you see a why you can bear any how." If you see a purpose you can accept meaningless pain. There was no meaning to the holocaust but purposes beckoned: to escape the Nazis, to find a country, a new home, and a new job, to save my parents, to write, to support a new family.

Purpose, meaning, faith—these are religious concepts. For a while I struggled with them on my own. But by and by I found help, for me the right kind of help. The first stepping stone of my religious journey was finding a church community.

After my two-year stint in New York with the Voice of America, Judith and I returned to Berkeley and were reunited with Max. Once more he had found a job for me, this time as an editor at the University of California, the job I held for twenty-five years, until my retirement. With the help of Judith's two brothers we bought a small house for our growing family. Our second daughter, Claire, was born during our stay in New York. We also acquired an honorary grandmother, Cousin Irma, whom we rescued from her lonely exile in London. Irma, in her sixties, worked as a maid in England (the only way for her to escape Nazi Austria). She had survived the war and the blitz. In 1948, I helped her join our budding but financially insecure family in California. We were richly rewarded by her playing a grandmother's role to our children. Without being consciously aware of it at the time, I tried to relieve my survivor guilt by doing for my elderly cousin Irma what I no longer could do for my parents. The fact that my mother, whom I couldn't save, and my cousin, whom I brought to America had the same first name helped me work through my guilt feelings.

In Berkeley, Max's house and my house were within walking distance of each other. Max rebuilt his den for a desk with two typewriters. Our wives did not resemble the types of our youthful fancies, and our dream of living in houses next to each other, with our children playing together, surrounded by our dogs à la Norman Rockwell, did not come true. Our families were friends in the conventional sense but never in the unique closeness Max and I had attained.

My older daughter Wendy, then five, began asking questions about God and Jesus, questions prompted by her playmates in kindergarten. We were looking for some kind of religious education for both our daughters. The Jewish community had no synagogue in Berkeley. It met in the local Unitarian church. We heard that the minister, Raymond Cope, was an extraordinary man and congenial to Jews.

Judith and I decided to investigate. The word "church" had painful connotations for me. It was the place where "they" went, and in Vienna "they" were the Christians, the Aryans, the anti-Semites, the Nazis. Although the Unitarian Church displayed none of the symbols and paintings of the churches I had seen in Vienna, I felt uncomfortable. As the minister stepped to the pulpit in his churchly robe I was ready to leave.

I cannot remember everything Cope said that morning, but I know he answered questions I hadn't even known to ask. He mentioned two images that immediately had significance to me. Every carpenter knows, he said, that wood has to be sawed with the grain, not against it, or he will get hurt. In the same way we have to live with the grain of the universe and not against it. He also spoke of a "gyroscope" we all carry within us that keeps its balance, no matter how much it is thrown off center. During the past years I had been thrown off center so many times that it was good to be reassured that something in us keeps our balance. I thought about the grain and the gyroscope. Where could I learn how to use them and how to live with them? I was in no way prepared to wrestle with those questions alone but felt Cope could help me.

This was the first time since I left Vienna that I was assured that there was an order in the universe, and that it was up to me to discover it and to live in accordance with it.

When I shook Raymond Cope's hand at the church door after that first service and he heard my accent, he asked me about my background. He said something to the effect that he hoped I would become active in his church, because as a Jew and a refugee I would have some special contributions to make to his congregation. And this after having been called a louse, spit on in the face, imprisoned, and unwanted by every country to which I applied for asylum!

Cope proved that he meant what he said. Not much later, he offered me the chairmanship of a committee that formulated the church school education. I told him that I had never been on any committee, much less a chairman, and that I knew nothing about religious education. He said, with convincing assuredness, that he knew I could do it. So I tried. I later was given several leadership positions. I conducted a Great Books group, headed the program committee, taught church-school classes, and finally served as a member of the Board, eventually becoming its president. Of course, I was scared. But Cope's unflinching confidence in me helped me overcome my self-doubts.

Cope found something praiseworthy in every religious faith. He stressed what they held in common rather than what was different. He credited Judaism with being the roots of Christianity and always spoke of "our Judeo-Christian heritage." He made me aware that the essence of Judaism lay in an ethic that had survived four thousand years of suffering, which included the destruction of their homeland, the diaspora, the Inquisition, pogroms, and the Holocaust. He made me see religion as a universal human longing for a reality that transcends the material world in which we live. We can approach this longing from many directions—Jewish, Christian, Islamic, Buddhist, Hindu, humanist, agnostic, even atheist.

Cope opened doors to areas which I did not know existed and which I was eager to explore. We discussed religion in many meetings, but we talked more about what true religion was *not* than about what it was. Religion was not a dogmatic set of rules. It was not a pyramidal structure with God, or the Pope, or a Chief Rabbi on top. It was not a promise of eternal bliss in Heaven or eternal damnation in Hell. It was not an area accessible only to special people but to everyone who earnestly searched for it. Religion was not a masculine hierarchy. It was not a belief system based on supernatural events. It was not a holy book written by God.

I wanted to find out what it was. I came to suspect that the key to that locked door was what Cope called "the Spirit of Life." Cope rarely used the word God. He spoke of the Spirit of Life. The term "spirit" had puzzled me since childhood, but it had remained at the periphery of my interest. In my childhood I was not concerned about matters that could be called religious. But now, in Berkeley in the late forties, having gone through the tribulations of my flight for life, I suspected that the Spirit held the key to religious mysteries.

In the Unitarian Church of Berkeley the Holy Spirit (or the Spirit of Life, as it was called there) was the center of the Divine Reality. But to me it still remained a hazy concept. When I asked what it meant, people again talked more about what it was not. It was not God as portrayed by Michelangelo and other artists. It was not a heavenly father. It was not a personal figure who performed miracles and answered prayers as Santa Claus answered children's requests. It was not something or someone residing in unreachable heights above.

But as my idea of the Spirit of Life developed, my marriage was in danger of becoming stale. Judith had married me for my potential. We both were successful in turning potentials into achievements. After the usual backbreaking jobs which were the apprenticeship for refugeedom, by the 1950s I had mastered the English language and was an editor at the University of California in Berkeley. We lived in our own home and were members of the local Unitarian Church. By this time we had three children and, for the first time since my emigration, had enough to live on.

But little to live *for.* Hitler was defeated, my parents dead, and the few surviving members of my family scattered all over the globe. I had looked up to Judith as my guide through the jungle of the American language and customs, and now I was able to speak and write in English. I was bored with my job. Judith stagnated with household chores, at which she wasn't very good. Lovemaking had become routine. The children were a delight, but constant talk about them was not as stimulating as the discussion groups at church. I began to look at other women, with their immaculate homes, their fertile minds, their intriguing bodies. It was the typical midlife crisis. That it was a wretchedness considered "normal" and almost expected, did not help either. It loomed over my midlife years as my shyness had loomed over my teens.

Then came the miracle.

Judith had been teaching Sunday school classes and was playing hymns on a little pump organ for the children in a children's chapel. While I approached religion with my mind, Judith approached it with her heart and through music. Perhaps this was part of our estrangement—our church life went in different directions. As chairman of the program committee, I made use of the rich resources of the University of California to find speakers for the Philosophers Club and for other intellectual discussions. I was only marginally aware of Judith's spiritual growth, which had taken her on quite a different path. So I was surprised when she asked me to attend a little ceremony she had arranged with the minister, Raymond Cope, and to which she had invited a few of her new church-school friends.

I attended, with some condescending skepticism, what Judith called her "conversion." I was suspicious that it would be some form of baptism, a changing from Judaism to Christianity. So I was relieved when the ceremony began with her declaration that she did not want to refute her Jewish heritage but rather wanted to expand her outreach.

With a magic that was his appeal to the congregation, Cope had worked out with Judith a ceremony that had the most unexpected consequences. Looking back, I would say it was the beginning of my conscious religious search. I became aware of the narrowness of my religious outlook. There was something that Judith said during that ceremony (although I don't remember the words) that opened a door to a world I never expected to exist, a world beyond reason and logic that had to be explored in order to become a fulfilled human being. Suddenly my religious horizon expanded. I realized that such an exploration was vital for me, although I knew even then that my search would have to follow a different course than Judith's.

It was one of those unexplainable moments of revelation. The rays of the afternoon sun hit the diamond in my ring and reflected the colors of the rainbow on the ceiling. In one flash, the prosaic little children's chapel was transformed into a shrine, the prosaic little pump organ became an instrument of glory, and my prosaic wife became a priestess. I hardly heard the words that she and Raymond Cope intoned, as he presented her with a silver chain and a pendant that combined the Star of David with a cross.

Even now I cannot think about that moment without becoming emotional. I saw myself as part of a great wholeness. It changed my view of myself, of Judith, of the world. Once more I could look up to Judith as my teacher, not of the American language and customs but of the potentials of a new and unsuspected dimension. A new dimension was added to our lovemaking as well, a spiritual quality that could almost be called worship, in the literal sense of the word—having great "worth."

Looking back I see that Judith's conversion converted me in a different way. It gave me an insight into what love is in its deepest sense. Love is often trivialized as kindness, helpfulness, companionship, emotional sustenance, or passion. Or it is elevated to a goal unattainable for mere humans, such as unconditional love for everyone, even one's enemies. In that little children's chapel, I saw a love that clearly had its roots in spirituality. It came close to being unconditional but was attainable by humans.

I dimly remembered having experienced something like unconditional love before, as a child, when I had felt the safety of my father's hand leading me through life, and I saw my mother as my source of comfort and security, offering me the nourishment and softness of her breast. But this, I realized, had been the infantile love of a child who hadn't faced the realities of life. Now I was an adult, having experienced the chaos and injustices of the world which had destroyed my childhood's faith in unconditional goodness and love. I regained a glimpse of this kind of deep love at Judith's conversion, and experienced it as the love of a mature person.

This emotional high did not, and could not, stay at that intensity. It faded but has never left me and, in fact, is growing again in old age. I have the strange feeling, which may well not be shared widely, that true love emerges only after all the emotional urges and physical needs have subsided. I can love Judith unconditionally, with all her faults, shortcomings, and irritations. This is a love not gratifying emotional and physical needs but fulfilling spiritual meanings.

Max, a devout atheist, found the effect of Judith's conversion on me difficult to understand. He was one of those whom the Holocaust had turned into a cynical nonbeliever, while it had turned me into a searcher for a divinity that made sense to me after my experiences in an absurd world. We had long discussions about the nature of God. As Max often said, he lived not according to the Bible but according to Webster. Editing was his religion, and the phrase "In the beginning was the Word" meant just that—the word, as Webster defined it. He could not see beyond Webster's definition of God as the Supreme Being. He saw God, as Michelangelo had painted Him—a man with a white beard doing magic. And the cross, even if united with the star of David, as Judith wore, was to Max the symbol of a tradition that too often had been the basis for anti-Semitic excesses.

On the topic of religion we agreed to disagree. In his later years Max hesitantly came to accept Webster's second definition of God as "eternal and infinite spirit." This definition was much closer to my own. Max found his spiritual nourishment not in churches or synagogues but in nature and his spiritual expression not in scriptures but in poetry.

It seemed to me that the Spirit of Life was everywhere, above, below, within us, and outside us. It was the stuff of life like the air, and just as difficult to hold. It was a source of strength and comfort. But what was it really? I was an editor and wanted a definition.

Logotherapy

My successes had done much to restore my self-confidence. Cope believed in me, many church members expressed appreciation for my activities, Judith saw me as a reliable guide in our lives together, the children held my hand in trusting belief as I once had held my father's hand, Max saw me as a valuable partner in our writing endeavors. But deep inside I remained unsure. In 1963 my daughter Wendy gave me Viktor Frankl's book "Man's Search for Meaning." Only when I became familiar with Viktor Frankl's affirmative philosophy was I able to solidify a worldview that made sense in my life, with all its ups and downs, all its blessings and horrors.

Frankl's philosophy had saved him during the three years in concentration camps, an experience much worse than my own. It rested on three pillars. First, that life has meaning under all conditions, even the most hopeless ones. Second, that every person has an innate will to meaning, which brings more fulfillment than the will to pleasure, power, or riches. And third, that one always has the freedom to find meanings, either by changing a meaningless situation where this is possible, or by changing one's attitude where it is not.

This was an existential philosophy whose time had come in the hedonistic and affluent America of the sixties! Existentialism was in vogue among the Berkeley students and spread from there throughout the country. The French existentialists, novelists like Sartre and Camus, became widely popular. The German existentialists, theoretical philosophers like Martin Heidegger and Karl Jaspers, were translated into practical use by Frankl who had proven, in his concentration camp years, that everything could be taken from you, except your healthy core, your spirit, and its resources of which your will to meaning is the strongest.

All that became clearer in the years to follow. What I saw in the sixties, when I became familiar with Frankl's ideas, was the puzzling realization that many of the evils in Hitler's Germany could be found, in much milder form, under the claim of "freedom" and "progress," in contemporary America. Families were shattered because they moved across the continent, even abroad, in search of more remunerative jobs. Married couples divorced, children moved out right after high school, grandparents lived their own lives, in independent loneliness. The three-generation extended family under the same roof, or at least in commuting distance, as I had experienced it in Vienna, hardly existed in America, at least not in the cities.

In Germany, the debasement of human beings took the harsh form of slave labor, exploiting people until the last drop of usefulness was squeezed from them. Efficiency was considered the highest value. I saw a trend in that direction in the United States. People were reduced to things to be manipulated for economic or political advantage. Nazi Germany worshipped power as the primary source of meaning and neglected the spiritual aspects. I saw the United States, which had been founded as a spiritual nation, beginning to drift in the dangerous direction of power worship.

Frankl distinguished two kinds of spirit—the human and the Ultimate Spirit. The human spirit exists entirely on the human level. It is part of the human make-up and contains a "medicine chest" of health-promoting resources—the will to meaning, goal orientation, purposes to fulfill, love beyond physical and psychological needs, a conscience beyond the superego, self-transcendence (the reaching out beyond our own interests toward others), self-distancing (looking at ourselves from the outside with a sense of humor), finding meaningful attitudes, and "saying yes to life in spite of everything" (the title of Frankl's first German book after his release from concentration camps). This was a definition of spirit I could understand and accept. It was not, however, what Cope had called "Spirit of Life" or what my maid Minna had called "Holy Spirit."

Ultimate Spirit was closer to the religious concepts of Cope. It existed in what Frankl called a "suprahuman" dimension. This was not, as he emphasized, a superhuman dimension, *beyond* the human, but rather *supra,* a higher dimension only because it included all other dimensions—the human as well as animal, plant, and non-living.

I talked with Frankl about these puzzles when I drove him to speaking engagements in California and when we hiked on his favorite Alpine mountain, the *Rax*. It took many walks on the *Rax* and many years of groping until I came to conclusions that made sense to me. I wanted to understand how these two kinds of spirits related to each other—the human spirit which enables us to sniff out the meanings of the specific moments of our lives, and the Universal Spirit where Ultimate Meaning, which is true for everyone, lies hidden. I felt that our human spirit could lead us to the Universal Spirit, but I didn't know how.

Frankl explained the connections with a metaphor. All our individual responses to the meanings of the moments, he said, run in the direction of Ultimate Meaning and converge there, just as the lines of perspective in a drawing run toward and converge in its vanishing points, even though the points themselves are not in the picture. In a similar way, he pointed out, every time we find a truth on the human level, or do an act of justice, create beauty, or practice love, we add one more line that will guide us toward Universal Truth, Ultimate Justice, Eternal Beauty, and Unrestricted Love, or to use the traditional term (which he didn't), to God.

In his concept, each moment offers us a meaning opportunity, most often trivial: to get up in the morning, to get dressed, to eat breakfast, to drive safely, etc. Then there are moments of greater impact. I experienced them when Judith was upset with me and I told her I loved her, when Wendy was frightened and I hugged her, when Max needed a ride to the hospital and I canceled a visit to the theater and took him. Often we can see the meanings of the moment clearly. Our conscience tells us, and our laws and customs guide us because these meanings are the tested reactions to standard situations. But the really important meanings of the moment are uniquely ours and often unclear. We know only later whether we have made the right choice. Examples from my own experiences include my decision to leave Vienna and emigrate to an uncertain exile, my marriage to Judith after knowing her for only two months, our decision to have a child. My search for meaning in the many moments of my life led me from a doubter to a believer in the existence of Ultimate Meaning, and I saw my shattered world come together.

The most questionable of Frankl's basic assumptions was his claim that we have the freedom to find meaning under all circumstances. What freedom did he have to make meaningful choices in the concentration camps? Where were my choices when the Nazi occupation of Austria robbed me of everything that had been meaningful to me? Where were my choices in the Brussels prison cell or in Merxplas? Where was my freedom to choose a country where I could build a new and meaningful life? It seemed to me that I had been tossed from one meaningless situation into another.

This emotional resistance was broken when I realized that Frankl did not say that we always have the freedom to change a meaningless situation but that our freedom lies in finding a meaningful attitude in the meaningless circumstances we cannot change. I was touched when Frankl, on one of our mountain wanderings, assured me that the meaning found through our attitudes in meaningless and unavoidable situations is the highest of all. When we find meaning by doing and experiencing, he explained, we change the world around us. But when we find meaning by triumphing over adverse situations, we change ourselves. We become better persons. How I soaked up these words after my unavoidable sufferings of the past years!

I learned that we can sniff out meaningful attitudes in meaningless circumstances in Merxplas, where many of the inmates were able to switch from a desperate and unanswerable "Why me?" to a challenging, "What can we do now, in this seemingly hopeless situation?" I was alive because I had used the resources of my spirit—my goal orientation (to survive), to see a purpose (to establish myself as a writer again), to self-transcend and help others I loved (my parents, my cousin Irma, Max). Although I did not always succeed, these resources gave me the strength to overcome obstacles.

I wanted America to know about this existential philosophy as a warning and a prescription for spiritual health. This philosophy made me look, for the first time, at my future with hope, rather than at my past with despair. It seemed to be the right philosophy for America, which was a young, future-oriented, optimistic country. It certainly was the right philosophy for me whose life seemed to have lost meaning and needed to find new guidelines.

I wanted Frankl to write a book for Americans in a language appealing to the intelligent laity and to establish an institute to teach and train people in logotherapy (therapy through meaning). He didn't want to do it and encouraged me to write a book and establish an institute myself. I accepted the challenge. After all, I was an editor and could write. Although I had no experience in running an institute, I had chaired a committee and eventually a Board. I accepted the challenge and it changed my life.

When I established "sharing" groups at the *Viktor Frankl Institute of Logotherapy,* I learned about the many miseries people suffered, and how they dealt with them, often quite successfully. Group participants, forced to suffer in meaningless situations, found ways "to turn tragedies into human triumphs."

A photographer, after an accident, had to lie in a cast for months. He later commented on his experience: "I became a much better photographer. When I lay in bed and could move nothing but my eye balls, I learned to see details which I had never observed."

In Japan, I met a ten-year-old American girl who had to bear what I considered a most pitiful handicap. She was born without a colon and had to wear three bags to collect her body wastes. When I asked her how her life was different from the lives of her classmates, she had to think for a moment. Then she said "*They* have to go to the bathroom."

One of our best logotherapists, when still in high school, broke his neck in a diving accident that left him paralyzed from the neck down. When he was released from the hospital he wrote to Frankl (typing with a mouth stick), "The accident broke my back; it did not break me." The young man finished high school, went to college, received his degree in psychology, and is now counseling clients, especially paraplegics.

Members of sharing groups learned from each other, and sometimes in unexpected ways. One woman explained how she handled procrastination. "When I keep postponing something I don't want to do, I start cleaning the house, which is what I hate to do worst of all. Then the other job does not seem so bad any more." There came the voice from a woman in a wheelchair: "Oh, how I wish I could do housework again!" A lot of learning occurred in the group because of that remark.

Many people felt defeated by their life situations but discovered unique solutions, often in exactly the areas of their defeats. Blind people found they could help other blind people better than any therapist. Quadriplegics saw themselves as models for other quadriplegics, whom they were able to show by example that meaning was still available. A patient in a cancer ward who had been diagnosed as incurable, said, "If you think I'll spend the brief time I have left feeling sorry for myself you have another think coming." He went from bed to bed cheering up other patients.

A woman who had survived the concentration camps wore a charm bracelet with a number of baby teeth. She explained, "This tooth is from Jakob, this one is Miriam's, and this is Susy's. They all died in concentration camps." When asked how she could live with such memories, she simply said, "I am now the director of an orphanage in Israel."

Any tragedy, small or large, could be a teacher. A woman told the group that she had been devastated when her husband left her. After the divorce was final, she found that she enjoyed her independence. She made new friends and developed skills that she didn't know she had. A man who lost his father when he was a boy was proud of becoming "a man" at an early age and helping his mother take care of his four younger siblings. A woman who grew up without playmates had become a novelist because "I invented the people I didn't play with as a child." A famous singer credited her big nose, about which she was teased as a child, for spurring her to make a special effort to train her voice and face the public.

Many group participants took divorce, death of a loved one, a miserable childhood, uncaring or abusive parents, and other past disasters as excuses for their present failures. They emphasized what was wrong with them. They learned from others who took the same past disasters as challenges and who focused on what was right in their lives. It may seem that tragedies are necessary for people to find meaningful directions. But this, of course, does not have to be. No one has to look for suffering to find meaning. But when suffering occurs and cannot be avoided, one can learn from it.

During this time I began to understand Divinity as a universal force rather than a father figure. I also began to understand another great puzzle. Why is there evil in the world?

One answer to this question was given by the Book of Job. For a long time I found God's answer to Job evasive. God told Job, "Who are you to ask such questions? Where were you when I created the world?" The answer seemed evasive as long as I saw Divinity as a personal deity. When I saw it as an omnipresent force which humans cannot fully comprehend, it made sense. I finally gained a glimpse of understanding about why the Creator does not and cannot be expected to intervene in certain miseries we experience on Earth.

Miseries which insurance companies call "acts of God" are indeed part of the creative process. We know now that earthquakes, tornadoes, and volcanic eruptions are consequences of geological, thermodynamic, stratospheric, and other forces. We know that many diseases are caused by microbes which are just as much part of the life cycle as we are, needing to feed on other organisms to survive. We know that the miseries of old age and death are due to the natural breakdown of all living things. These are not punishing or arbitrary acts of God but part of the Creative Order. There is the possibility, even likelihood, that the Divine does not stand above that order but *is* the order, which was not created for the benefit of individuals but for the benefit of life itself.

These evils caused by "acts of God" were easy to explain. I found it incomparably more difficult to explain to myself human-caused miseries like the Holocaust. But explaining Holocaust-like evils was exactly what I was trying to do, at least to my own satisfaction. The answer came from evolution.

Human beings have evolved to a stage in which they have free will. In Frankl's terminology, we have been given the spiritual dimension to say No to our animal drives. In the metaphor of the Fall from paradise, our ancestors decided to say No even to God.

Matthew Fox, the Oakland theologian whom I heard in the Berkeley Church, does not see the eating of the forbidden fruit as disobedience to God but rather as a courageous response to a challenge. Fox understands the myth of the Fall to mean that, before our "original sin," humans were just another form of instinct-driven animals. They were given the precious but dangerous gift of free will. This was a tremendous step forward, and Matthew Fox called it not Original Sin but Original Blessing. Such a view places women in quite a different light. Eve becomes the archetype of the creature who opened up the dimension of the human spirit and was courageous enough to accept the gift of free will and its consequences.

The interpretation of the Fall as Original Blessing helped me understand the existence of human-made evil. It is the direct consequence of our freedom to choose. Human-made evil exists where humans decide to choose to act evil. The Holocaust and the evils we see committed all over the world were not God-inflicted but the result of human choices that went against the "grain of the universe," against Ultimate Meaning, against the ecosystem, against the "will of God," against a caring Life Force.

Life offers us the potentials for good and evil. It is we who choose. It is time we stop blaming God and the Devil and accept responsibleness. We have grown up from being children, holding on to Father's hand. We are adults and have to accept accountability for our own actions, bow our heads, and accept those "evils" that are the natural consequences of the Divine Order.

I admit that this is a simplistic explanation. Things are probably much more complex. Maybe we are still too close to our jungle ancestors and not ready to use our freedom primarily for the good, for "going with the grain." Maybe the human race, in order to survive, has to develop a few more evolutionary steps until we have gained the responsibleness that goes with the proper use of our free will.

In 1965 I returned to Vienna with Judith. I hoped to exorcise the evil done to me and my family. I had ambivalent feelings. This was the place of my youth, which beckoned after all these years. Forgotten were the agonies of my teens, the boredom of the school years, the self-doubts, and anxieties. I immersed myself in the atmosphere of familiar songs, music, theater, Viennese food, and Alpine meadows and flowers. But it was also the place of humiliation, expulsion, and murder. And these were not forgotten.

I had the strong urge to face the places of my traumas—the university where I was beaten, the street corner where I had to clean the sidewalk of anti-Hitler graffiti and was spat on, the apartment that was taken from us, the railroad station where I said good-bye to my parents. I wanted to meet my classmates again. I had spent eight years of school with them, and then I had seen them on the street with swastikas in their button holes. They had looked the other way. I had made contact with one of my classmates, and he had sent out invitations for a get-together in a restaurant. At graduation we had been a class of twenty-two. Only eight still lived in Vienna. Seven showed up.

I tried to have a frank discussion of the Nazi period, but there was that usual denial of having known anything until it was too late. One of them had that self-pitying reaction so typical of the Viennese. "You refugees had it good. You were safe in America. You cannot imagine what suffering we had to go through—the bombing, the war, the starving!" When I reminded him that he didn't have to lose his parents in concentration camps, he sighed and admitted regretfully that, yes, "Excesses did happen."

How often have I heard Austrians say, "All this happened years ago. Why don't you forgive and forget?" My answer was: forgive, yes, but never forget. We mustn't forget and let the world forget, so that this evil will not happen again. Actually, I wasn't sure about the forgiveness part either. How can I forgive cruelty to others? It seemed to me that only the injured party has the right to forgive.

Reconciliation is another thing. It doesn't mean that I forgive and forget but that I can live with the memory. I have seen too many refugees obsessed with the cruelties and injustices they have endured. They reject anything German, including the language, the music, the songs, the literature, the landscape, and everything that once had been precious. It seemed to me that they are giving Hitler a post-mortem victory by letting him mar their lives. I found reconciliation necessary so I could continue with my life.

Children Finding Their Own Ways

Judith and I really never cut our Jewish roots, but our joining the Unitarian Church sometimes seemed like a betrayal. None of my three children had a Jewish upbringing, although they were aware of their Jewishness and the high demands of Jewish morality. They, too, haven't left the Jewish tradition but, like myself, reached out beyond it. The Unitarian hymn book contains a hymn with the line "Roots hold me tight, wings set me free." This line means much to me. Our roots are Jewish, but we want the freedom to reach out for the truth wherever we can find it.

Wendy's search for a fulfilled life led her to various oriental religions and finally to a cult which called itself TIC, The Inner Core. Some members claimed that it meant The Inner Christ, a phrase that made me uncomfortable. For me Jesus Christ was more Jesus, the Jewish prophet of high insight and morality, than Christ, the Messiah for a new faith and the unintentional source of anti-Semitism.

I could accept the way Wendy explained TIC to me—the belief in the existence of a universal life force within us. This was close to Frankl's belief in the human spirit, which is our healthy core, and to my own concept of the Divine Reality. I had to admit to myself that TIC, whatever the letters stood for, was a cult. Wendy's association with it ultimately led to her death.

Wendy met Ron there and fell in love. We received glowing phone calls from both of them. They decided to get married, applied for their marriage license, bought their wedding rings, and were planning to come north for us to meet him. A few days before their planned trip, Ron strangled her and then shot himself. We will never know what happened. It was an incomprehensible and senseless murder. Even after all I had lived through, this was the worst blow of my life. Why did she have to be taken from us at the young age of forty-three? Only when I was able to change that unanswerable question to a grateful, "How lucky we were to have had her for forty-three years!" could I find comfort and relief.

Claire followed our own footsteps, staying closest to mine. She married Rich Bradley, who had a Methodist upbringing. Both are now active in the Unitarian Church of Davis. She is well aware of her Jewish roots, is familiar with Jewish rituals and symbols, has been in Israel twice, and understands some Hebrew. Her interest in Judaism was kindled by a visit from Israel of Judith's cousin Ruth, who spent her husband's sabbatical year at the University of California in Davis. Claire, at that time, was mourning Wendy, and Ruth became a sister substitute.

Our son Richard follows his own spiritual paths. He appreciates his Jewish roots and has taken the oral history of our family on tapes, having interviewed me and Cousin Irma, who had her own story of surviving the Holocaust. If anything in Richard's beliefs comes close to religion, it is his faith in astrology. Right now, he is spending hours in libraries studying the religions of the world, trying to find his own.

Strangely enough, I learned about the essence of Judaism in the Unitarian Church. Raymond Cope spoke about the wisdom and high morality of the prophets and related their teachings to our daily lives. He read the poetry of the psalms and the stories, which were no longer fairy tales but parables about problems I had experienced. In the Unitarian Church I found the first tentative answers to religious questions, which made me see my life, with all its tortures, in a light that was beginning to make sense.

Many of my Jewish friends have asked me what comfort I find in a church, and I am certain my parents would have asked that question too. I have had periods of doubt and guilt, and many moments when I felt I was on a blasphemous path. I recalled past episodes, like the one in the Brussels prison cell when I pounced onto the columns of ants following their leader on the floor, killing them by the hundreds while some survived in little dips on the ground. Or a moment in the shipyard when I observed a moth stuck in the mud. I had the power to kill it, let it struggle, or liberate it. Was this how God worked? By accident and whim?

I have often had conversations with my father and mother while sitting in church, in silent meditation.

"What are you doing in a church?" Father asks.

"I have asked myself that question many times," I say. "At first, I felt uncomfortable. The hymns. The organ. The pastor's robe."

"What changed?"

"Nothing. Except me. The way I see things now. I have learned what religion is. Mama, you are a very religious person."

"I? I hardly ever went to the temple."

"Going to a temple doesn't make you religious. It doesn't matter where you are but what you are. When Wendy was about eight, a neighbor

was suspicious of Unitarians because they don't believe in the Trinity nor in the divinity of Christ. She asked Wendy whether God was in the Unitarian Sunday school, and Wendy answered, 'Yes. He is there if I bring him along.' She had learned in a year what took me twenty."

Father has his doubts. "God in a little kid?"

"In all of us. And everywhere else. It makes more sense to me than a God who worries about the plate you eat from or whether it's pork."

"There were good reasons for these rules," Father points out.

"Yes, three thousand years ago. Things have changed. We have changed. Rules are for kids. We have grown up, perhaps too fast. But it's time to find our own rules."

""The Nazis found their own rules, and look where it's gotten us." Father's voice rises and his face turns red, as it always did in arguments.

"Maybe that's what Wendy meant when she said she brings God along," Mother mediates. She becomes anxious when Father's face turns red.

"Yes," I say, grateful she understood. But I am desperate at my own limited understanding, "I haven't come to grips with the Nazis," I admit. "They are part of reality. It would be a great help if God would pick up evildoers and stick them into hell. But that's not the way it is. Reality has its horrible sides. We have to fight evil where we can and accept it where we can't. And learn not to repeat it."

"And what does your Unitarian God do about it?" Father still sounds bellicose.

"I don't know," I admit. "People who claim to know what God is are worshipping an idol. God is unknowable."

"The Jews knew that four thousand years ago," Father says. "That's why they forbade making an image of Yahweh and even pronouncing his name. But they knew well who Yahweh was. There was no other God besides him. There was no shilly shallying."

We sit still for a while. I don't want to point out that Yahweh did nothing to prevent the Holocaust or to stop it. Evil Hitler had to be stopped by brutal force, another evil. Perhaps it's time to rethink the idea of a personal God high above. The God within Wendy, and everyone else, is not a man with a beard in heaven.

"God may not have any shape or form," I say out loud. "Not the master of the universe but the fabric of the universe itself, and we all are part of it—people, animals, plants, rocks, the air, water. Perhaps he is not a he, nor a she, but an omnipresent It."

"But does 'It' care?" Mother tests cautiously.

"You're right," I admit. "That bothers me, too. We need a God who cares. A God who is part of love and hope, wisdom and justice."

"That's a lot of rationalization," Father decides.

"But what comfort to be part of a whole, woven together in a web of life!"

"That's very poetic," Mother says. "Bubi, you are a poet."

I glory in her praise. "But also very practical. I wish I'd known this when I was alone, forsaken, driftwood. . . ."

"A moth in the mud," Mother adds.

"Yes." I am surprised and pleased that she knows. "Part of a web in a universe that cares."

"The Unitarians teach you that?" Father asks suspiciously.

"Not exactly. They don't teach by telling. They let us grope for answers that make sense to each of us, individually."

"And that's the answer you found?" Father probes.

"I'm still groping. I'm getting new ideas. And discarding some old ones."

"You discarded Judaism?"

"No, Judith and I are Jews and always will be. You don't have to give up your faith to become a Unitarian. You add to it. But I have discarded the idea that God is a He. Or a She. It's a force, a creative energy."

"An energy that loves?" mother suggests.

"Something like that. But church is more than a place for speculations. We do practical things. We carry out the demands of the universe for love and caring. We collect money to feed the hungry. We sometimes

let the homeless stay overnight in the church building. We brought Vietnamese families over, refugees as I was, and helped them get a new start. We brought over some people from Tibet who had to flee their country. We adopted a sister Unitarian church in Transylvania when it was threatened by communism. There is so much love to spread around. Terrible things are happening."

"And God?" Father now smiles.

"God needs a little help from us." I smile, too. A warm feeling is spreading among us. Like in Vienna.

"We have to care for each other like a family," I say. "In Vienna, we met every week, in coffee houses. In our homes. We helped each other in emergencies. Celebrated together. We do that in church, too. The web of the family has expanded."

"An extended family," Mother nods. "We know how it feels when the family is shrinking, when one member after the other is deported. I am glad you found a new one, Bubi, in your church. But why didn't you go to a synagogue?"

"I've often asked this myself," I admit. "Sometimes I think I made a mistake. But this church has done so much for us. It helped us both to grow."

"You are happy here," Mother says. "That's the main thing."

It was like a blessing. I needed that.

In 1972 I had one of my happiest experiences when our first grandchild, Heidi, was born to Claire and Richard. This was the beginning of a second generation of my American family. As I looked at her through the window of the nursery in the Sacramento hospital, I realized that I was the ancestor of a new tribe! How I would have liked to share this moment with my mother!

Here was Heidi, in a hospital room full of infants. She was by far the prettiest. The nurse picked her up for me to see her better, and a daydream flashed through my mind.

Mother joins me.

"Look, Ma," I greet her, "I'm a grandpa!"

"You made me a great-grandma," she marvels. "And I haven't even met my grandchildren. You are starting a new family here."

"I'm the only one to do it," I tell her. "Everybody else was wiped out."

But she is in no mood for sadness. "I remember when you were born. Not in a hospital. Babies were born at home then. Dr. Bachrich delivered you. He delivered all the babies of the family. Your birthday was a holiday for us all. Everyone came. Our bedroom was crowded all day long. We had been waiting for you, so long. Seven years. They all peeked into the crib. Your cousin Schorschi was quite upset. He had his Bar Mitzvah *that year and wore his first suit with long pants. But no one paid attention to him. You were the center."*

She knocks at the glass window as she used to knock on wood for good luck. "Hello, Heidi. Things are different. The family is gone. We were about twenty-five or thirty, meeting on birthdays and holidays. Where are they all?"

"Maybe they are all gathered, somewhere," I say, not really believing it. "Maybe they see her."

"Yes," she agrees. "Somewhere and somehow. Maybe just in your head. Maybe in Heidi's head, when she grows up."

"Or in her genes," I add, knowing Mother doesn't know about genes.

But she knows in her own way. "Heidi," she says. "I come from the nineteenth century. Your father lives in the twentieth. You are reaching into the twenty-first. You're the future, Baby. Keep it going!"

Heidi became my next teacher, and so was her sister Shala, who was born three years later. In my lectures I had often talked about uniqueness as one path to meaning and had told my listeners that one could find uniqueness in personal relationships to a parent, child, or friend.

I experienced my uniqueness in my relationship with Heidi. I became clearly aware of it when she, at that delightful age of three, called out, "Follow me, grandpa!" and I followed her, doing what she was doing—hopping, skipping, running, falling on the floor. I felt rather foolish. At the same time I was conscious of a happiness that was hard to explain on a rational basis. Heidi was very inventive and thought up childish games which I, in my sixties, shared with her. I was proud that I was the only person she asked. These were meaningful moments, for her and for me.

I learned from my grandchildren to live in the moment. They didn't worry about past or future. They lived completely in the present. I remember one specific incident. I saw Shala sitting very still on the lawn, staring intensely at the grass before her. I couldn't see anything in particular. When I bent down to her level, I saw a tiny inchworm climbing up a blade of grass. That inchworm absorbed her full attention.

This reminded me of an incident in my autograph-hunting days in Vienna. I had managed to sneak by the reception clerk of the Hotel Bristol, where the Indian philosopher Rabindranath Tagore was staying. The door to his room was wide open, and I saw him sitting in front of a little table, concentrating on a bouquet of flowers in a vase.

He was a holy-looking man with a white beard. I dared not approach him. He finally became aware of my presence and kindly asked me to come in so he could sign my autograph book. He, too, had observed some little insect, as did Shala fifty years later. I was struck by the thought that a three-year-old child shared the wisdom of living in the moment with a great philosopher.

When Shala was born, I could not imagine how this newcomer could ever become as precious to me as Heidi. Yet, after a few weeks the mystery of unconditional and undeserved love became clear to me. Here was existential proof that it existed, that love and caring were part of the grain of the universe. By her mere presence, her giggle, her smile, her grip of my finger, Shala took her place in my heart, next to Heidi.

I had heard from many of my clients how important grandparents can be to their grandchildren, giving them attention, understanding, and guidance. I myself had no such experiences. Three of my grandparents had died either before I was born or when I was very young. The fourth, my mother's mother Ida, was an arrogant, selfish woman to whom I never got close. But now, with Heidi and Shala, I experienced the grandparent relationship from the other side. It has been a source of joy and fulfillment.

When my granddaughter Shala was twenty-two she became interested in the Davis Baptist Church and, after a few weeks, converted to Christianity and became a Baptist. This was a severe test of whether my life philosophy, which I had pieced together over many years, stood on solid ground. Was it in the best interest of a person to find his or her own guidelines? Should I have been stricter in bringing up my children in the Jewish tradition? I was satisfied that the words in that Unitarian hymn expressed my true beliefs—that I kept my roots in Judaism and Unitarianism gave me the opportunity to reach out beyond. This had worked for Judith and me and, to some extent, for my children. But now my grandchild had broken with her Jewish roots and reached out for beliefs that were foreign to me.

Shala and I had always been close. When she was about ten, she told her mother, "I like grandpa because he never lectures me about what to do. He asks me what I want to do, and then talks to me about whether I really think that's the best way."

I was proud that she felt that way. But had I overdone my liberal ideas? Perhaps children need strict guidelines until they are mature enough to find their own. How old do children have to be before they are able to find their own directions? Was the notion correct that even small children intuitively know the "grain of the universe" and, if left alone, will find their unique ways to live within it? Or are they empty vessels into which adults pour their own beliefs, wisdoms, and prejudices?

In the Unitarian Church I had met people who came from a variety of religious backgrounds. Those with a strict Catholic upbringing seemed to find it difficult to switch from a vertical to a more horizontal religious belief system. Catholic homes and schools had given them a firm religious foundation, which most of them found sheltering for the rest of their lives. But those who found it confining had a hard time freeing themselves from their early schooling.

In my logotherapy groups I had met many people who suffered from "noetic" depressions caused by a value conflict between a vertical religious or parental upbringing and the horizontal views of their present spouses and peers. I have a Jewish friend from my high-school days who had told his son he would never see him again if he married a gentile girl. This showed me how far intolerance can go.

Can tolerance also go too far? Had I been too tolerant in the upbringing of my children? Joiner Wendy had become part of The Inner Christ cult, and Richard was playing with astrology. I could accept that, especially the way they interpreted their beliefs. But now Shala had converted to a religion that sought salvation by the Jewish rabbi Jesus in whose name Jews had been persecuted for two thousand years.

I spoke to Shala and to some of her new Baptist friends. They surrounded her with love that radiated from their unshaken belief in the man Jesus, whom they firmly believed to be divine. They got comfort and security from their belief in a vertical structure of Reality that led from them, through Jesus, to a Father God in heaven.

Shala was a bright young woman, but so vulnerable, so unsure of herself! So ignorant of her strengths, so hopelessly groping for meanings and goals! I could identify with her. I, too, had felt unsure and vulnerable in my young years. I, too, had been sheltered by the love of my family, and it had turned out not to be enough. I had seen my family shattered. I had needed a more permanent anchor and found it after an arduous but rewarding search.

Shala had found it in a belief system that was different from mine. It was her way of tuning in on the creative life force, and if she found fulfillment and security in the beliefs of the Baptist doctrine, I could accept that. Judith and I, Shala's parents and her sister, we all surrounded her with our human love and security. Shala will have to find her suprahuman permanent sources herself. What she has found now may give her permanent answers or may be a launching pad for further search. I trust her to find her way.

Perhaps my naive optimism blinds me against the realities of life, as Max often argued. But I still believe that the meaningful life has to be found through a tireless personal search. This search may lead each person in different ways, over different way stations, toward a common goal. Some people find their direction through guidance, others by torturous search. The religious outlook is "right" for the person, as long as it checks with his or her experience and does not harm the searcher or others.

Is my acceptance of Shala's conversion a mere rationalization? An attempt to force Reality into the straitjacket of my preconceived notions? With the vertical view of my early years, I would have seen Shala's conversion as a defeat for my philosophy of life. In my present horizontal outlook I am able to see it as a challenge for her to find her own way.

The Wisdom of Hindsight

Retirement was not a time for sitting in an easy chair. It was a time of lecturing, seminars, workshops, and writing about what was really meaningful to me. Our work in logotherapy took Judith and me all over the United States, Canada, Europe, Japan, Israel, and Mexico. We made friends, some of whom have kept in touch with us over many years and even have come to visit us now that we no longer are strong enough to travel to far-away places.

I made an astounding discovery. While most of my past activities withstood the scrutiny of hindsight, some events have lost their original glamour. The first sale of a story to a well-paying American magazine now seems irrelevant. The triumph I felt ghostwriting a speech for Earl Warren, Chief Supreme Court Justice, has paled. The power I felt after being elected president of a six-hundred-member church is no longer a source of jubilation. These had been important for my ego but not for my soul.

On the other hand, there were incidents I paid little attention to at the time that I am now proud of. A man told me that my seminar saved his sanity. Others have come to thank me for writing something in my books or articles that changed their lives. I was touched to receive a bouquet of flowers from a woman in Germany who credited me with preventing her suicide. I do not recall what I did or said, but these incidents were testimony that I had learned from my painful experiences and that something good had come from evil.

Life had been good to me for a long time, but Wendy's murder in 1986 was a heavy blow. I have often speculated what would have happened *if*. If we had persuaded Wendy not to move to southern California where she met Ron. If we had been with her when it happened, talked things out, or physically prevented him from attacking her. Such fantasies only leave me frustrated. I come back to the irreversible reality and my feelings of guilt.

Our lives consist of thousands of Ys. When we come to a fork in the road, we must go either right or left. If we made a mistake, we cannot go back and take the other path. We only have the opportunity of choosing again at the next fork. But there comes a last fork, when there are no more choices.

"There still are choices, Dad," Wendy says. "Don't be sad."

"I have trouble believing in an afterlife," I tell her. "What choices are left?"

"The ones you talked about in logotherapy. You cannot wish me alive again. The choices are now within you. You can be sad or accepting. I know you find it hard that I am no longer among the living. But you can go on with your life. Your family needs you. Your friends need you. You still have much to do."

"But we all miss you so terribly much. There is a tear in the fabric of the family that can never be mended. We'll never see you again."

"Oh yes, you will. I'm with you always."

"Memories? That's true. An incidental word overheard or the shape of a woman in the distance, and you are with me. A whole little scene from the past flashes by, with you in it. But I can never hug you, talk to

you, or hear your unexpected answers. All your answers in my fantasies are my own. How I would like to know what happened! How you came to die."

"This I cannot tell you. It happened. The why is not important."

"To me it is. I keep asking myself, 'Why?' Is there a reason?"

"I believe so. And you believe it too, Dad. You believe in an Ultimate Meaning, where everything hangs together and makes sense. Not on a human level. What looks like coincidence and willfulness to us, may be part of a pattern on a higher level. Like an earthquake or a tornado. These things are catastrophes for us, but they are part of nature. Nature has its own rules. They are not made to please us. We are not the centerpieces of the universe."

"But you are dead! Gone forever. I keep asking myself if I could have done anything to prevent it."

"Please, don't. You and Mom have done your best, believe me. Perhaps you made mistakes, but never on purpose. The same is true for me. I didn't let myself be killed on purpose. Things happen."

"They can be prevented," I argue desperately. "If you could go back far enough, you would see where the mistake was made. If you only could go back to that crucial Y in the road. Perhaps we should have brought you up Jewish. With the stricter guidelines of tradition."

"No point in torturing yourself, Dad. I had a good life, searching for my own guidelines. I needed that freedom."

"But look where it led to!"

"The last two months were the happiest of my life," Wendy says quietly.

"But at what price!"

"Happiness is not measured by time. Who knows what would have been in store for me. Nothing and no one can take these two months from me. They are stored forever."

"These are words in a book. In fact, in Frankl's book. They are arguments in my head. I need comfort for my heart."

"Don't sell your head short, Dad. You're a head person. Mom and I could get 'unknowable' information through intuition. You have to get it through logic"

"That's much harder."

"No, just different. Remember how excited you were when you read in von Ditfurth's book that the atoms present at the birth of the universe, fourteen billion years ago, are still with us? That was a scientific discovery, acceptable to your head."

"Yes," I allow. "It's astonishing to think that an atom that was in Socrates might be in me. But it's no comfort."

"Just wait. Isn't it a logical bridge to immortality? Isn't it possible, if physical atoms are immortal, that there might also be atoms of the spirit that survive and live forever? That an atom of Socrates' spirituality may be in you, too?"

"Yes, I have thought about that. But I get little comfort from that head trip. If bits of your spirit live on somewhere in the universe, I can't hug them, talk to them, love them. I wish I could believe in an afterlife the way so many people do. A place where we can meet again."

"Perhaps you will, in a form that we cannot imagine. We just don't have the capacity to see the whole picture. Just as an ant can't see our reality, we cannot see the reality more highly developed creatures would be able to see. Or reality as it really exists. Remember what von Ditfurth says: We are the Neanderthalers of human evolution. Your friend Frankl says it in different words. There is Ultimate Meaning in a dimension we cannot yet enter. Your Unitarian Church says it in still another way: We are part of the fabric of the universe which includes areas unknowable to us."

"I cannot draw comfort from these speculations. They are the rationalizations of people who do not want to accept the cruel truth that we die and that's the end of it. We look for happy endings where there are none."

"We talked about that before, Dad. Sometimes the happy endings are within us."

"Nothing can change the fact that you were taken from us at the age of forty-three."

"And nothing can change the fact," Wendy replies, "that we were together for forty-three years."

Just as my daughter Wendy lives on in my memory, my parents live on in memory. The seeds they planted have come to fruition. My father lives in me through his love for order and logic, his common sense, his humor. And my mother through her creative imagination, her gentle understanding, and her patience. I am sorry I didn't know them better. I know that at the core of their relationship were trust, love, and hope. I am lucky to have duplicated these treasures in my own marriage.

Most of my childhood memories seem to be of my father. It is his face that still haunts me when I remember our goodbye at the Vienna railroad station in 1938. We all bravely pretended that our separation was only temporary, but Father knew better. When the train began to move out of the station his face shattered like glass. This I shall never forget.

The memory of my mother is of a different sort, and the emotions are deeply buried in me. They surface when I see mother-son scenes in a movie or a play. Then tears begin to flow. Father-son encounters in movies don't have the same effect. This, too, puzzles me.

On our logotherapy tours in Europe, we always combined our lectures and seminars with concerts, theaters, and sightseeing. On mother's hundredth birthday, we were in Paris. We visited Heinrich Heine's grave and wandered around the crowd on the square of Montmartre, looking at the paintings displayed by the artists. We sat down in one of the open-air restaurants and ordered dinner. In a spurt of sentimentality I ordered a bottle of champagne and filled our glasses.

Mother joins us. She is more wrinkled and bent than I remember her. I know a few old ladies in Berkeley who are in their nineties. Some don't hear or see well, many use walkers, some are confused. Mother is fine, just smaller, shriveled.

I lift my glass. "To one hundred and twenty," I toast her, in the Jewish tradition of birthday wishes.

She looks at me with affection. "I'm glad you could afford to visit Paris. I was worried you would struggle. Three children!"

"We are doing well, Mama," I assure her.

"And you have taken in Cousin Irma."

"She's a great help, a substitute grandma. None of our children has grandparents."

"Her name is Irma, just as mine," Mother says.

"That's a bit of trouble," I confess. "Sometimes I resent her. She's alive, and you aren't."

"Don't look at it that way. I wouldn't be alive now, anyway. A hundred years! She's only seventy-four. Make her feel part of the family."

"But she is, she is!" I assure her. "The kids love her. She spoils them just as you would. She lived through the London blitz and lost all her possessions. Including her photos. She needs a family."

"We all do." Mother sighs, bobbing her head as old people do. "Irma had tough luck. Her husband and daughter both died of TB. Terrible."

"I know. She talks of them often. And how glad she is to have a family again. Only I wish it were you. That we could spend birthdays together, the way we did in Vienna. Including this one."

"I'm here," she said. "I will always be with you. I promise."

A flower vendor approached with a basket of red roses. She was as wrinkled and bent over as my image of Mother. Only she was real.

"I'll take all the six bunches in the basket." I handed the old woman some francs. "One I keep, the others are for you."

She peered at me over the rim of her glasses, smiled, and shuffled on. I handed the bouquet to Judith. She understood.

As the film of my life is now in its last reel, I look it over. There was a clear break between the first part in Europe and the second part in America. Two sets of families, two cultures, two epochs. Only memory ties them together. It is comforting to see the two as a unity.

The players are different, the scenery is different, I am different. Yet, there is continuity. Without being aware of it, I have dragged some of the old family rites and rituals into my new life. They help me see my life as one meaningful totality. Perhaps this awareness of wholeness is also the purpose of rites and rituals in a culture.

Although I didn't plan it, many of the old rites and rituals of my family in Vienna have emerged in new forms in my American family. I was not aware of the continuity until recently. I only knew I felt good at these events. Even the number of people in the new core family has grown to nearly the size of the one that perished. With the help of my wife's two brothers and their offspring, our birthday celebrations bring together about fifteen people. In contrast to my European family, these are mostly young people. I was the youngest in Vienna; here I am the head of the clan. As we did in Vienna for birthdays and anniversaries, we meet in the celebrant's home—not in walking distance, but an easy commute by car.

These gatherings focus on the young. We meet in their parents' home, and new rituals include a swim in a pool or a soak in a jacuzzi. A common card game is still a must. Not the Viennese tarock, but the Californian "Oh, Hell," a game enjoyable for adults as well as children.

Thanksgiving is celebrated in our son Richard's house, Christmas with daughter Claire and her husband and children.

To avoid the modern habit of clawing off elaborate wrappings and looking briefly at a gift before tearing open the next, we have invented a new ritual, Spin the Bottle. We arrange the gifts in a circle. Then we spin a bottle. The person whose name is on the gift the bottle neck points to opens the gift. Everybody has a chance to see the present before the bottle is spun again. Opening gifts lasts for an hour or more.

Elaborate dinners, formerly prepared by Viennese maids, have been replaced by potlucks. Thanksgiving dinners feature a ritual added by Wendy: Everyone around the table tells of events of the past year that he or she is thankful for. This is as close as we come to the former New Year's celebration of recalling the events of the year.

Family trips are not regular. However we did take one trip to Europe together. I introduced memorable places to my children and grandchildren. There are no wise old uncles and aunts to come to with personal problems, but we do meet from time to time in encounter groups to freely discuss our feelings toward each other.

Conclusion

Undoubtedly, Hitler brought about the severest tragedy of the twentieth century. If he had not existed, millions would not have died in the war he provoked and in the concentration camps he invented. He caused suffering for the millions more who were "lucky" to survive. Whole libraries of books have been written by survivors who could not get over the torments they and their loved ones had to go through. Emotionally, it has been impossible for me to really work through my losses and my pain, but I have had moments of pure rational thinking when I have been able to see even these cataclysmic murderers in some perspective. If Hitler had not existed, I would not have been exposed to the influences of the men and women who shaped me and my beliefs. If Hitler had not disrupted my life, I very well may have married one of those flashy, glamorous women I had dated in my days in Vienna. It may have turned out well. I don't know and never will. I do know that I would have never met my reliable life partner Judith and never would have had my children and grandchildren, the sources of so much joy. If Hitler had not driven us from our homeland, my friendship with Max would have lasted as it did. But it would not have been strengthened by the anguish of emigration and the Holocaust.

During the thousands of years of recorded history there have been other Hitler-like monsters, such as Ghengis Khan and Ivan the Terrible. They were responsible for the death and suffering of whole populations, but they had no lasting influence. Had they never existed, our lives would not be different.

Then I think of personalities who lived thousands of years ago whose influence on us is still strong. These are people of wisdom and high moral character like Confucius, Buddha, Moses, Jesus, and Socrates. This seems proof to me that the "grain of the universe" is toward the good and that people who go with the grain have a lasting impact. Those who go against it don't. It also seems proof, or at least an indication, that the grain goes with the positive, the caring, the constructive, the yes-saying. It is comforting to believe that Hitler will go the way of Ghengis Khan, and contemporaries like Albert Schweitzer and Mother Teresa will have the influence of Socrates and Moses.

It is, of course, very hard for people who have suffered at the hands of Hitler to take such a sweeping historical view. I am reminded of a dream I had after I received confirmation that my parents had died in the Theresienstadt concentration camp. I saw myself wandering through a jungle-like wilderness when a huge bird swooped down and picked me up with his claws. We flew up to the sky. I was not afraid but rather curious seeing the landscape from above. The bird carried me over a meadow with ditches full of corpses and skeletons, such as were shown in photos after the liberation of the death camps. As we circled, the ground began to change. The corpses turned into humus, grass started to cover them, flowers bloomed, trees grew, and the landscape became lovely. I woke up refreshed and needed no psychologist to interpret that healing dream. Perhaps, if we were able to find a bird that could show us a sweeping view of history, we would see that the good is fragile but lasting, and evil is powerful but ephemeral.